KW-013-634

DUGDALE SOCIETY OCCASIONAL PAPERS

No. 36

The Warwickshire Yeomanry in the Nineteenth Century: Some Fresh Aspects with a Transcript of the three surviving Troop Rolls

PAUL MORGAN, M.A., F.S.A.

THE DUGDALE SOCIETY
1994

© *The Dugdale Society 1994*
ISBN 85220 070 6

British Library Cataloguing in Publication Data. A catalogue
record for this book is available from the British Library

Printed in Great Britain by
Stephen Austin and Sons Ltd
Hertford

THE WARWICKSHIRE YEOMANRY IN THE NINETEENTH CENTURY: SOME FRESH ASPECTS

THE history of yeomanry regiments in general and of the Warwickshire Yeomanry in particular has been well publicised in this two-hundredth anniversary year.[1] What cannot be said, however, is that the history of our county regiment is well-documented, especially insofar as its ordinary members are concerned, so a fresh look at the sources available may not be inappropriate. Central records have details of commissioned officers, but not of the rank and file, so an investigation of these 'High-spirited young men, substantial householders, or their sons, whether farmers, tradesmen, or of any other occupation', as the original poster put it,[2] seemed worth undertaking. There is a tradition of volunteer military service to defend one's own locality going back to the fourteenth century[3] and the younger Pitt's suggestion in March 1794 for the formation of a 'species of cavalry consisting of gentlemen and yeomanry' for the internal defence of the country was soon acted upon, so that by the end of the year no less than thirty-two corps of yeomanry had been raised, of which ten survived until after the 1914–18 War.[4] In addition, at least nine independent mounted troops for the defence of particular towns and districts were formed in Warwickshire between 1795 and 1804.[5] These need further investigation, as for instance, one not noticed hitherto for Solihull, Knowle and Elmdon, begun in 1798.[6] The Atherstone troop was started before 1800, not 1803,[7] as its colours were consecrated at Mancetter parish church by James Chartres, master of Atherstone Grammar School, on 4 June 1800 and a sermon printed, dedicated to the Hon. Mrs Dugdale of Merevale and the wife of Abraham Bracebridge.[8]

The absence in central records of details of yeomen is reflected in the local ones; only two troop rolls in the regiment's possession and one among the Leigh archives deposited at the Shakespeare Birthplace Trust Records Office have been found, although there were eight troops in all between 1794 and 1894.

The surviving rolls conveniently cover the period between 1804, when the Volunteer Consolidation Act was passed,[9] and the formation of the Imperial Yeomanry in 1901[10] and Haldane's Territorial Army in 1907[11] when the organisation of the regiment changed radically.

Firstly, a word must be said about the officers; during the nineteenth century they nearly all came from the land-owning and gentry classes. However, a minority were professional men, such as Welchman Whateley, the Birmingham coroner, or William Wilmot, a Coventry lawyer.[12] Among the landowners can be found the titled magnates (the Earl of Warwick, Lords Aylesford, Willoughby de Broke and Leigh) as well as the ancient untitled families such as the Shirleys of Ettington, the Dilkes of Maxstoke and the Lucys of Charlecote. There is also a considerable proportion—41 per cent in the three surviving rolls—of the second and third generations of families which had made more recent fortunes. Some were local, such as W. C. Alston of Elmdon Hall, a brass tubes manufacturer, whose name is commemorated as the Alston-Roberts-West family of Alscot, G. F. Muntz of Umberslade (metal rolling) and Darwin Galton of Edstone (banking and gun-making). From further afield (Yorkshire) came Edward Raleigh King of Chadshunt, and Frank Dugdale of Wroxall, whose wealth came from banking and cotton in Lancashire, and who married the only daughter of the 4th Earl of Warwick. The taking of a yeomanry commission was a recognised means of gaining an entrée into local society.[13]

The initial appeal in June 1794 to raise four troops of 54 men each was immediately successful and the total was increased during the next few years. The strength of the regiment at its annual inspection, held usually shortly before or after harvest, is recorded[14] (unlike the Worcestershire Yeomanry) and reflects the national political and economic situation. The reduction to only three troops in 1802 was immediately countermanded by the threat of invasion which, however, had disappeared by 1812. A rise in 1813 may have been due to the extension of regular cavalry pay to all yeomen prepared to undertake at least twelve days annual training;[15] up to that time they had been paid only when called out. The increase to 437 in 1831 from 287 in 1830 was caused not only by the political reform agitation then rife, but also by the amalgamation or disbandment of local troops and an official establishment laid down;[16] the Nuneaton and Warwick troops were the only ones then remaining.[17] The Chartist riots in Birmingham and industrial disturbances when the services of the Yeomanry were in demand were no doubt the reasons for the relatively steady numbers between 1838 and 1844.[18] The strain on the regular army imposed by the Crimean War led to a recruiting drive and a turn-out of 440 in 1854.[19] In 1862 four hundred men were on parade, the highest total reached during the nineteenth century; this military enthusiasm by the public was due to its suspicions of the hostile intentions of the French, reflected in the beginnings of the Volunteer movement.[20] It is interesting that the Worcestershire Yeomanry, which was always larger than Warwickshire's, in the first half of the nineteenth century had an establishment of 750–770, and between 1874 and 1900 of 430–530.[21] However, the period of agricultural depression from the late 1860s onwards combined with a lack of interest by the government in the absence of any invasion threat led to a steady decline in numbers, reaching a nadir of only 206 in 1881,[22] until the South African War. A slight rise after 1881 may have been caused by a recruiting drive by W.C. Paulet, colonel from 1880 to 1891. The changes brought about by the formation of the Imperial Yeomanry altered the character of the regiment and does not concern us here.

Each of the three surviving troop rolls follows the same pattern, beginning with the articles of enrolment. Those of the First and Second Troops are identical. As William IV is named as the monarch to whom allegiance was to be sworn, the rolls could not have been started before 1830. Both begin by quoting the Volunteer Continuation Act of 1802, enabling certain yeomanry and volunteer corps to continue their services, but in fact this Act had been repealed in 1804.[23] Then follow six conditions: 1) officers were to receive commissions from the King or Lord Lieutenant; 2) corps were to be embodied in case of invasion to serve anywhere within Britain and to suppress riots in Warwickshire or any adjoining county; 3) men were to receive no pay unless embodied and to attend mounted on a serviceable gelding or mare; 4) while embodied, men were to receive pay and be subject to military discipline; 5) men were responsible for their arms and accoutrements; 6) each man was to be subject to such penalties and rules agreed upon by the troop commander and take the oath of allegiance.

The Sixth Troop roll covers the years 1852 to 1868 and details fifteen articles exactly the same as those proposed by the Committee for the Management of the Subscription of the County of Warwick for the Internal Defence of the Kingdom in 1794, including the words 'His Majesty' and not 'Her' for Queen Victoria.[24] It would seem likely that these articles were circulated centrally from a government source, as similar articles were laid down for both the Worcestershire Yeomanry[25] and the Buckinghamshire Yeomanry.[26] They follow the tenor of articles used for the First and Second Troops with variant details, such as that pay would be as light dragoons if embodied, or if a substitute were sent to make up numbers, he must be from the county, of good character, accustomed to riding and approved by a majority of the troop, and that any pay received from the government by officers, or any other person, would be put in a common purse and divided equally among the troop.

Besides these articles, a single printed sheet issued about 1794 to members of the First Troop is in the Regimental Museum. One side lists details of uniform and equipment, subjects which have been well studied already.[27] The other side of the page gives penalties 'agreed to . . . for the better maintenance of good order', which appear to be rather high; a shilling was exacted for talking in the ranks or arriving late, and no less than 10s. 6d. for coming to exercise with arms or accoutrements dirty or out of order, with a guinea for the second offence. Fines were collected by the quartermaster and any surplus at the end of a year disposed according to the wishes of the majority of the troop. This sheet is accompanied by a printed pro forma filled in for 'Mr Low, yeoman' with an order to parade with the First Troop at the King's Arms, Kenilworth, on 27 December 1795 at 8 p.m. for duty throughout the whole night.[28] This call-out was previously unknown and may have been connected with the riot by the 5th Irish Dragoons at Stratford-upon-Avon on Christmas Day, when the Fourth Troop under Evelyn Shirley of Ettington helped to quell a disturbance.[29]

When this First Troop roll was actually begun cannot be exactly determined. Mention of William IV in the oath implies some time after June 1830. Entries are in four columns headed: Name; Residence (just the parish in most cases); When enrolled (the date of joining, not signing); When resigned. This last column was very irregularly maintained. The dates of enrolment suggest that it was begun about 1836–7. The first names were those of five officers who joined between 1822 and 1834, followed by sixty other ranks with enrolment dates between 1794 and 1836, in no particular order. Only about 30 per cent have the fourth column completed, though many entries are wholly or partially deleted, presumably to indicate resignation; a high proportion just have 'left' added. The imperfections of the record are underlined by the note 'thirteen names wanting' inserted about 1836. From that year until 1854 there are some 74 names in chronological order, then a blank until 1863, when the quality of the entries changes completely with the advent of Captain A. C. Pretyman as troop commander. A member of an old Suffolk landed family, his connection with Warwickshire is obscure; he gave Nuneaton as his place of residence and joined the county magistracy in October 1862.[30] A former officer in the 74th Highlanders and the 25th Regiment, the King's Own Borderers, he immediately reorganised the First Troop's administration. After enrolling himself, there are forty-eight names in order of rank with dates from 1830 and one from 1797, of which more later. This shows that besides the captain there were a lieutenant, a cornet, a quartermaster and sergeant-major, plus four sergeants and four corporals, two farriers, a trumpeter and a bandsman, as well as thirty-one privates; all after the trumpeter are given in strict alphabetical order. It has to be remembered that although ordinary cavalry soldiers were commonly called troopers, that style was not officially adopted until 1922. Pretyman commanded the Troop until 1869 and enrolled a further twenty-three men between 1865 and 1868, including another bandsman and a lieutenant. The Troop was recruited from an area roughly bounded by Birmingham, Solihull, Leamington and Nuneaton. Before

1831 members came mostly from the Hampton-in-Arden and Coleshill areas, with individuals from as distant as Long Itchington and Kenilworth. During the next thirty years there was an influx from Chilvers Coton, Berkswell, Bickenhill and Leamington, while under Captain Pretyman, eight joined from Nuneaton and nine from adjoining parishes. However, the roll ceases with the advent of the 7th Earl of Aylesford as troop commander in 1868 and the return of Pretyman to his native Suffolk.

The Second Troop roll is considerably longer than the First and, although apparently dating from the same time, it continues until 1898. It contains 475 enrolments, including two double entries. Stylistically, it is very similar to the First Troop roll giving columns for the signature, residence, when enrolled and when resigned, though the last was rarely filled in before 1872, when W. C. Alston of Elmdon took over the command, held until 1901. The earliest enrolment date is September 1831, given for three men from Birmingham. There was a steady flow of recruits throughout, rising and falling as the numbers in the regiment varied. The Second Troop was known as the Birmingham Troop, originally led by Heneage Legge of Aston Hall, and the majority of men came from that town. Edward Bolton King, then of Umberslade, was captain from 1837 to 1845 and under him forty-five men came from that district, but there were also thirty-three from Tanworth-in-Arden and adjoining parishes. Bolton King was followed by Darwin Galton, then of Edstone, and although only eight enrolled from Birmingham, there were no less than twenty-seven from the Tanworth area during his command (1845–57). From 1857 to 1872 the Troop was led by Philip Wykeham Martin, of Bentley Heath and Packwood, when there were thirty-four enrolments, of which half came during 1861, reflected in the regiment's peak strength at the 1862 inspection. None was from Birmingham, except one from Handsworth; all were from Solihull and its neighbourhood, except one from Feckenham (Worcs.) and two from Henley-in-Arden. The fact that Martin was the only Second Troop leader during the nineteenth century who came from an old landed family, not having made a fortune recently in industry, may have had something to do with this.

Martin's successor was W. C. Alston, of Elmdon Hall, who came from a Birmingham manufacturing family. He was troop leader from 1872 until about April 1898 when the roll ends. The thirteenth and final vellum sheet was crammed full of signatures; indeed it had been very scrappily maintained throughout the 1890s. The South African War and the formation of the Territorial Army changed the regiment's organisation completely and were probably the cause of the roll's discontinuance. Notwithstanding the decline of regimental numbers during the last three decades of the century, no less than 245 men enrolled between 1872 and 1898 at a fairly steady rate—84 between 1872 and 1880, 97 from 1881 to 1890 and 64 between 1891 and 1898. Of these 29 per cent gave Birmingham as their place of residence and another 21 per cent came from its suburbs, most of which were mentioned, with eight from Handsworth, three each from Moseley and Sutton Coldfield and two from Edgbaston. There were also representatives from nearby industrial districts not in Warwickshire, such as nine from West Bromwich, three from Smethwick and two from Dudley. Another 20 per cent came from the Solihull area, including Henley, but none from Tanworth-in-Arden; very few omitted completing the place column. Among these Frank Soulby, who, enrolled in 1876, kept a sports shop in Turl Street, Oxford; his local connection, if any, has not been discovered.

The Sixth (or Stoneleigh) Troop roll is among the Leigh archives deposited in the Shakespeare Birthplace Trust Records Office, which suggests that further rolls could be among family papers, but none has been located. It contains 159 enrolments between 1852 and 1868. It was probably begun in 1854 when the regiment was reorganised into eight troops,[31] although the first thirty-one names are all dated 25 March 1852 and the next thirty-five in April-July 1852. The remaining ninety-three enrolments vary between one and ten a year, with surges to nine in 1853 at the time of the Crimean War and ten in 1863, when the regiment reached its maximum strength. The change of troop leader from Edward Chandos Leigh to the Earl of Craven in 1867 was the reason the roll ceased to be kept. Not surprisingly, the greatest proportion of men, 45 per cent, came from the

Stoneleigh area; 23 per cent came from the Coventry/Nuneaton district and 11 per cent from near Rugby. There were also four men from Birmingham/Smethwick, six from Watergall and individuals from Stratford and the Leighs' other house at Adlestrop (Glos.).

A popular concept of yeomanry regiments was that they were 'run by fox-hunting officers with fox-hunting farmers as troopers'.[32] The 19th Baron Willoughby de Broke wrote that when his father took over command of the Fourth Troop in 1863, he led into Warwick for the annual training fifty-four 'Prosperous, well-fed and well-wined' troopers, all his tenants and each mounted on his own horse.[33] Significantly, this was the time of the regiment's greatest strength; but was this a fact, or merely nostalgia for an idyllic rural past? The 1794 Committee's poster appealed 'to substantial householders, or their sons, whether farmers, tradesmen or of any occupation, who are willing to enrol'.[34] A rather unscientific survey of the 841 men on these three surviving troop rolls, representing possibly 8.5 per cent of those who passed through the regiment during the nineteenth century, enables an estimate to be made of 518 (62 per cent) of their occupations, based mainly on contemporary directories and local histories. Farming families are inferred from the occurrence of the same surname in the parish at the appropriate period. Ordinary labourers and workers are not listed in these sources and it can be assumed that the 323 unidentified men belonged to these classes; it is perhaps significant that all except two[35] were sufficiently literate to sign their names and write their place of residence. Practically half (49 per cent) of those identified were farmers or came from farming families, and another 15 per cent followed trades serving the agricultural community, such as two cattle-dealers, four corn-merchants, seven black-smiths, twelve dairymen and six saddlers. Another large group (19 per cent) was concerned with food and drink, including twenty-seven inn-keepers, sixteen butchers, ten bakers, seven brewers and nine wine or beer retailers. Among the 6 per cent craftsmen were three coopers, three bricklayers and eight shoe-makers. With the high proportion of men from Birmingham and Coventry in these troops, the manufacturing industries (6.5

per cent) are well represented, including three button-makers, four iron-founders, two ribbon-manufacturers and miscellaneous trades such as a dog-collar maker, a mathematical-instrument maker, a photographer and a bicycle-saddle maker. Similar proportions of men were involved in various retail trades and smaller numbers in offices (five insurance agents, three lawyers and two stockbrokers). Less usual occupations include a possible portrait painter, the keeper of an asylum for juvenile delinquents, a bird-dealer, a goldsmith and a besom-maker. One can only say that, if this small portion from three out of the eight possible troops were typical, the regiment was served by a good cross-section of the county community, animated, it is to be hoped, by loyalty to country.

The Manchester and Salford Yeomanry, responsible for the notorious Peterloo massacre on 16 August 1819, has been analysed in great detail.[36] The occupations of eighty out of its 101 men in 1822 showed thirty-nine occupations, compared with 111 in the Warwickshire troops during the whole century, which is not surprising in view of the multitude of trades followed in the industrial Midlands:

	Percentage of Yeomanry Occupations in	
	Manchester	**Warwickshire**
Tradesmen	45	27
Professional & Business	23.7	16
Craftsmen	22.5	9
Manual Workers	7.5	8
Farmers	—	49
	98.7	109

The excess in the percentage figures for Warwickshire is accounted for by the fact that sixty-nine of the men had two occupations such as builder and timber-merchant, farmer and cattle-dealer, inn-keeper and coal-merchant. Presumably the absence of the agricultural element in the Manchester Yeomanry reflects its urban catchment area.

A defect of using directories as sources is very obvious when comparing rural with urban areas, since only the owners of premises and masters of businesses were mentioned. Thus, 80 per cent of the men from Tanworth-in-Arden who enrolled in the Second Troop between 1834 and 1863 can be identified; there were fifteen farmers, two butchers, a blacksmith, a landowner and a jobmaster. W. J. Sheldon, a farmer from Earlswood, is a good example. He was troop sergeant and a prominent local personality, treasurer of the Tanworth Association for the Prosecution of Felons in 1869, the year he won the prize for the best horse in the regiment, and a member of the North Warwickshire Hunt. In contrast, only 41 per cent of the occupations of the Leamington men who enrolled in the First Troop between 1794 and 1865 can be traced—two millers, father and son, an insurance agent, a baker, a plumber, a gentleman and a farmer, though possibly the trumpeter and the two bandsmen were professional musicians. Even fewer Coventry men can be identified—only nine of the thirty-two enrolled between 1816 and 1868: two farmers, two auctioneers, a lawyer, a shoemaker, a ribbon-manufacturer and a lawyer's son, later connected with the Rudge bicycle firm. However, the proportion whose occupations are estimated is so small that one wonders if deductions are valid; it can only be asserted that apart from the fact that agriculture is well represented, the remainder seem to have been a good cross-section of contemporary society.

The fourth column in the rolls of the First and Second Troops is headed ' When resigned' and was very imperfectly maintained; no attempt at all to record these details was made on the Sixth Troop roll. In the First Troop, resignations were noted between 1837 and 1847 and then none till Captain Pretyman arrived in 1863. Occasional resignations were entered in the Second Troop roll between 1875 and 1891, but thirty-one entries in the First Troop and twenty-eight in the Second just have 'resigned' or 'left'. Of men who do have a date, 32 per cent served for three years, 15 per cent for four, 13 per cent for two and 10 per cent for one. Those who served for seven or more years account for 15 per cent. Some men were in the regiment for very long periods; the record must be held by Robert Brown, a Coleshill farmer, who first joined in 1797 and signed the roll a second time in 1863 when sergeant-major under Pretyman. He may have resigned shortly after 1863, as Colonel Griffiths remarked at his inspection in 1864 that he was pleased to find fewer old men in the ranks compared with his previous inspection ten years before.[37] Three men served for thirty-one years, such as John Burbidge of Coleshill, who enrolled in 1808 and resigned in favour of his son in 1839.[38] Besides resignations, thirteen deaths and eight transfers were recorded. Many entries have a line drawn through them presumably indicating resignations.

Between 1873 and 1894 ten men, mostly from Birmingham, were recorded as deserters from the Second Troop. Presumably they missed attending the annual training for two consecutive years, as two men were recorded elsewhere as being dismissed in 1890 for this reason, and were fined £9 each.[39] In May 1898 a local paper reported that an unnamed yeoman was arrested and marched through the streets of Warwick, escorted by a sergeant and two troopers with drawn sabres, to appear before Colonel Lord Willoughby de Broke, when a fine of £2 was imposed and dismissal from the regiment.[40]

Commissioned officers served for long periods. For example, when the fifth Earl of Warwick died in 1893, he had held a commission for fifty-four years.[41] Similarly, Edward Bolton King was in the Regiment for fifty years.[42] Lieutenant Pettit of the Wiltshire Yeomanry, although incapable of performing any duties, was still Adjutant of the regiment when he died aged eighty-two in 1836.[43] The majority of the Warwickshire Yeomanry officers served for eight years and upwards.[44]

The main purpose of a yeomanry regiment was to help maintain order within its county, or other area. In September 1800, for instance, there were bread riots in Birmingham when the First and Second Troops were called out to assist the 17th Light Dragoons.[45] What was not previously known is that there was also trouble in Stratford-upon-Avon at the same time. Joseph Hill, a wigmaker who kept a chronicle of local events, described how 'the yeomen came into town to do regular parading the streets; towards morning they dispersed' and four days later the

Yeomanry guarded prisoners sent to gaol.[46] He also noted when annual inspections were held in Stratford; in May 1801 he recorded 'The Yeomanry came to Stratford for six days and were reviewed by General Greenfield and gain'd great applause; It has been a very hot week.'[47] Later, in June 1807, he reported 'The Yeomanry cavalry came into town and behaved very ill'.[48] He also noted that Sir Charles Mordaunt gave the Yeomen a dinner at Walton, presumably when the Fourth Troop was temporarily disbanded.[49]

In May 1824 following the repeal of the Combination Acts there was an outburst of rioting which caused the Yeomanry to be called out for a week[50] and George Lucy, the squire of Charlecote, reluctantly left the London house he had taken for the season.[51] The last time the Yeomanry was called out to aid the civil power was during the Chartist troubles of 1848.[52]

A word must be said about the regiment's ranking in the army hierarchy, where yeomanries come immediately after the Honourable Artillery Company and before the Volunteers. Since 1885, the Warwickshire Yeomanry has been listed as the second senior yeomanry after the Royal Wiltshire; although this position has been to the regiment's advantage—in the 1939–45 war, for instance—it is not strictly accurate. This order was based on the supposed foundation dates of regiments with a continuous existence and which had never been disbanded for a period. The Worcestershire Yeomanry, for example, had been disbanded between 1828 and 1831, and seniority was reckoned from the re-commissioning. However, the 1885 table was carelessly compiled and influenced by correspondence with individual colonels who were not entirely disinterested. No less than thirty-two troops of yeomanry were raised in England in 1794,[53] so the exact date of acceptance by a Lord Lieutenant is crucial. The Warwickshire Yeomanry was commissioned by the King on 16 June 1794, and this makes it sixth in seniority, with the Pembrokeshire Yeomanry (22 April) and the Royal Buckinghamshire (8 May) only slightly older. Locally, however, 25 June 1794 is regarded as the real foundation date; on this day a meeting was held in Birmingham that resolved to raise four troops of 54 men each[54] and this is thus the anniversary commemorated in 1994.

It may not be inappropriate here to mention a few of the more notable Warwickshire yeomen. The only man on the surviving rolls to have achieved mention in the *Dictionary of National Biography* is Chandos Wren Hoskyns (1812–76) of Wroxall,[55] who was a lieutenant in the Second Troop between 1845 and 1851 and was on duty at the Chartist troubles in Birmingham in April 1848. He was a copious writer on agricultural affairs, advocating reform of land tenure, remarkable for his wit and humour.

An early member of the Second Troop was Thomas Welch, a currier and patten-tie maker of 15 Bromsgrove Street, Birmingham, who lived in the Bristol Road. He issued six variants of a penny copper token with a spirited representation of a mounted yeoman, similar to Edward Rudge's plate published in April 1800, loyally inscribed round the edge 'Armed to preserve (*or* protect) our lives, property and constitution against foreign and domestic enemies'. It was engraved by I. G. Hancock, considered 'pre-eminent' among producers of tokens and who was employed by Matthew Boulton at the Soho factory.[56] Welch does not appear on the roll, so he would seem to have resigned before it began. He may have been the man of this name who in 1858 bequeathed £200 for the poor of St Luke's, Bristol Street, Birmingham.[57]

The only literary connection of the Yeomanry in the nineteenth century seems to have been Isaac Evans of Griff, the brother of George Eliot; he enrolled in 1836[58] when aged twenty. Estranged from his sister on account of her liaison with G. H. Lewes, they were later reconciled. He became a land and estate agent and mining engineer. Edward Coleman of Birmingham who enrolled in 1838[59] was possibly the portrait artist of 15 Old Square and a well-known member of the Royal Birmingham Society of Artists, though the possibility that the yeoman was his son cannot be ruled out.

An unusual character was William Wilmot (1808–60), a Coventry attorney who enrolled as a cornet in 1834 and was promoted lieutenant in 1841.[60] He was a reactionary Tory and supported the Coventry weavers in their struggle against the introduction of steam-power. He was very popular with the ribbon-weavers and it was probably a relief to his fellow officers and professional colleagues when he died in 1860, shortly after resigning his commission and during his term of office as Mayor of Coventry.

There were at least two notable trumpeters during the century. The earlier was J. W. Walker of Meriden, who enrolled in 1825, when aged fifty; he was a music teacher, born in Hanover, and presumably was one of the Germans who followed the Georges to this country; he died in Meriden in 1856.[61] The other trumpeter was the remarkable John Spicer, who served in the Third Troop in Warwick for over thirty years and who had been on duty with the Yeomanry during the Chartist riots in Birmingham in 1839. He was a saddler and harness-maker at 33 Jury Street, Warwick, but he was primarily a naturalist and taxidermist; Spicer is a famous name in the latter occupation. He was also an inventor who made a spun-glass jacket, worn at a Yeomanry ball, and a pioneer photographer. However, in 1866 he was on parade with his troop outside the Warwick Arms, in High Street, Warwick, where the officers' mess was located until 1884. His horse took fright as the trumpeters were sounding and he fell, striking his head on a kerb. He was left partially paralysed and died after a short period.[62]

Shakespeare realised that a period of soldiering was part of many men's lives; Jaques in *As You Like It*, makes the fourth of the seven ages of man that of 'a soldier, Full of strange oaths, and bearded like the pard' before settling down as 'the justice In fair round belly with good capon lin'd' and this seems to have been the progress through life of many yeomen.

Whether these sidelights on the history of the Warwickshire Yeomanry during the nineteenth century are of much value in view of their incomplete basis is debatable, but a most important aspect has been left to the last, and that is its social importance. Commissioned officers would be accepted into county society without question regardless of wealth. For other ranks there is little documentation, but the comradeship and social ties can be inferred. Charles Griffin, farmer and miller of Chesterton, sergeant and later quartermaster in the Seventh Troop, when pulled up by Captain Edward Raleigh King for some deficiencies in his drill, replied 'Look here, captain, I've been a yeoman twenty years and you are not going to make a soldier of me now'.[63] When William Fairbrother, a grazier of Burton Hill Farm, Burton Dassett, the last of his line and a long-serving yeoman, fell ill in July 1914, his landlord and former troop captain, the 19th Lord Willoughby de Broke, would go and sit at his bedside regularly.[64] The fact that a high proportion of yeomen served for long periods in a purely voluntary body implies friendship and comradeship. Indeed, this strong bond of comradeship among the yeomanry, that has persisted to the present day, is probably the most important aspect of its history.

NOTES

Abbreviations in Notes and Index

HAA   H. A. Adderley, *History of the Warwickshire Yeomanry Cavalry* (Warwick, 1912).

HAA 1896, *History of the Warwickshire Yeomanry Cavalry* (Warwick, 1896).

Q.L.   F. B. T. Money Coutts, 5th Baron Latymer, *The Yeomanry Cavalry of Worcestershire, 1794–1913* (privately printed, 1914).

[1] *Year of the Yeomanry, 1794–1994*, 1994 and *Liberty, Loyalty, Property: an Exhibition of Treasures of the Yeomanry 1794–1994, Christie's . . . London . . .1994*, Army Museums Ogilby Trust, Winchester. The historical perspective is given in Ian F. W. Beckett, *The Amateur Military Tradition, 1558–1945*, Manchester, 1991; comprehensive details can be found in Peter D. Athawes, *Yeomanry Wars: the History of the Yeomanry, Volunteer and Volunteer Association Cavalry*, Aberdeen, 1994. HAA is the standard regimental history.

[2] Warwickshire County Record Office, CR 229/16/2.

[3] Beckett, p. 8.

[4] G. Fellows and B. Freeman, *Historical Records of the South Nottinghamshire Hussars Yeomanry, 1794 to 1924*, Aldershot, 1928, pp. 325–34; reprinted in Athawes, pp. 147–62, but *cf.* the comments on pp. 21, 35, 67–8.

[5] Athawes, p. 179, lists no less than 17 troops in Warwickshire between 1794 and 1802, but it is not clear whether all were mounted.

[6] Warwick C.R.O., CR 781; illustrated in R. Pemberton, *Solihull and its Church* (Exeter, 1905), facing p. 31.

[7] HAA, p. 23.

[8] James Chartres, *A Sermon Preached in the Parish Church of Mancetter . . . before the Loyal Atherstone Volunteers of Cavalry and Infantry . . . the 4th Day of June 1800 being the Day of the Consecration and Presentation of their Colours*, Atherstone, 1800.

[9] 44 George IV, cap. 54; Beckett, p. 100; Q.L., pp. 225–8; this Act repealed three earlier ones.

[10] 1 Edward VII, cap. 14; Q.L., pp. 230–31.

[11] 7 Edward VII, cap. 9; Q.L., pp. 231–34.

[12] P. Searby, 'William Wilmot of Coventry', *Warwickshire History*, vol. 3, no. 5 (1977), pp. 61–9.

[13] Beckett, p. 189.

[14] HAA, Appendix C.

[15] Beckett, p. 120.

[16] HAA, pp. 50–1.

[17] HAA, pp. 21–2.

[18] Beckett, p. 137.

[19] HAA, pp. 80–1.

[20] HAA, p. 85; Beckett, pp. 166–72.

[21] Q.L., pp. 221–3.

[22] HAA, p. 103.

[23] 42 George III, cap. 66; printed in Athawes, pp. 138–42; repealed by 44 George III, cap. 54; Q.L., pp. 225–6.

[24] Warwick C.R.O., QS22/Easter 1795; another copy, CR16/27.

[25] Q.L., pp. 5–7.

[26] Ian F. W. Beckett, *Call to Arms*, Buckingham, 1985, p. 30.

[27] L. Barlow and R. J. Smith, *The Uniforms of the British Yeomanry Forces 1794–1914; part 9: Warwickshire Yeomanry*, Tunbridge Wells, 1987; H. F. A. Strachan, 'The Uniform of the Warwickshire Yeomanry to 1914', *Journal of the Society for Army Historical Research*, vol. 44 (1966), pp. 114–23.

[28] In the Warwickshire Yeomanry Museum; *Liberty, Loyalty, Property . . .* no. 16.

[29] HAA, p. 13.

[30] C. W. Deacon, *Warwickshire Court Guide*, London, 1888, p. 142.

[31] HAA, p. 79.

[32] Raymond Carr, *English Fox-hunting, a history*, London, 1976, p. 179.

[33] Lord Willoughby de Broke, *The Passing Years*, London, 1924, p. 43.

[34] Warwick C.R.O., CR 229/16/2.

[35] Nos 48, 86.

[36] Beckett, pp. 135–7 and references there cited.

[37] Nos 6, 149; HAA, p. 87.

[38] Nos 63, 104.

[39] HAA, p. 116.

[40] *Stratford-upon-Avon Herald*, 20 May 1898.

[41] HAA, p. 128.

[42] HAA, p. 99.

[43] 7th Marquess of Anglesey, *A History of the British Cavalry, 1816 to 1919*, London, 1973, p. 78 note.

[44] HAA, Appendix B.

[45] HAA, pp. 27–8.

[46] Roy Palmer, 'Joseph Hill, his Book; the Diary of a Stratford-upon-Avon wigmaker', *Warwickshire History*, vol. 4, no. 6 (1980/81), pp. 197–8; Shakespeare Birthplace Trust Records Office, PR 117 (photocopy).

[47] S.B.T.R.O., PR 117, p. 70; HAA, p. 29.

[48] S.B.T.R.O., PR 117, p. 77; HAA, pp. 38–9; *cf.* Elizabeth Hamilton, *The Old House at Walton*, Salisbury, 1988, pp. 46–7.

[49] S.B.T.R.O., PR 117, p. 80; HAA, pp. 32–3, 35.

[50] *V.C.H. Warwickshire*,VII, p. 295.

[51] Mary Elizabeth Lucy, *Mistress of Charlecote*, London, 1983, p. 37.

[52] HAA, pp. 73–4.

[53] An authoritative discussion and lists are in Fellowes and Freeman, Appendix D; see also Note 4 above.

[54] HAA, pp. 1–6, 10–1; Beckett, p. 75.

[55] No. 321; HAA, pp. viii, 74.

[56] W. J. Davis, *The Token Coinage of Warwickshire*, Birmingham, 1895, nos. 23, 47–52.

[57] *V. C. H. Warwicks*, VII, p. 566.

[58] No. 51.

[59] No. 253.

[60] No. 4; HAA, p. viii; see note 12 above.

[61] No. 65.

[62] *Heartland of Warwickshire Recorder 1989*, p. 20; information from Allan Jack via Ms Pam Copson.

[63] Sir Charles Mordaunt and W. G. Verney, *Annals of the Warwickshire Hunt, 1795–1895*, vol. 1, London, 1896, p. 250.

[64] Ibid., p. 325; Willoughby de Broke, p. 44.

EDITORIAL NOTE

The First Troop roll is written on one side of five vellum sheets, and the Second Troop roll on thirteen sheets sewn to form rolls; the Sixth Troop roll consists of a single vellum sheet with enrolments in two columns on both sides. Entries have been numbered 1–851 for ease of reference.

[ ] editorial suggestions for faded or rubbed entries
( ) parts of an entry ruled through in pencil

*   an entry written in pencil
** an entry in pencil but later overwritten in ink

Names and places in the first two columns are shown as written; dates in the third and fourth columns have been put in a standard form.

THE ROLL OF THE FIRST TROOP OF THE WARWICKSHIRE YEOMANRY
commonly called the Vellum Roll, c. 1836–1868

Warwickshire Yeomanry Museum, Warwick
Reproduced by permission of the Trustees

Articles of Enrolment of First Troop of Yeomanry Cavalry for the County of Warwick

We whose Names are hereunto subscribed in pursuance of an Act of Parliament passed in the Forty second year of his Majesty King George the Third entitled 'An Act to enable His Majesty to avail Himself of the Offers of certain Yeomanry and Volunteer Corps to continue their Services' to voluntarily enrol ourselves in the Corps of Cavalry called the Yeomanry of the County of Warwick formed for the Internal Defence and Security of the Kingdom, on the following conditions:

The officers to receive Commissions from his Majesty or from the Lord Lieutenant of the County, or others who may be especially authorised by his Majesty for that purpose.

The Corps to be subject to be embodied in case of Invasion, or an appearance thereof, or in case of Rebellion or Insurrection and to be marched to any part of the Kingdom of Great Britain, and to be subject to be called upon for the suppression of Riots or Tumults within the County of Warwick or any adjoining county.

To receive no pay, unless when embodied or called out, but to attend mounted on a serviceable Gelding or Mare to be approved by the Commanding officer of the Troop, for the purpose of Exercise at such times and places as shall be fixed by such Commanding Officer.

In all cases when embodied or called out on Service, to receive pay as allowed by Government and to be subject to Military Discipline, as the rest of his Majesty's regular and Militia Forces.

Such Articles as are furnished by Government and shall be

allowed to each man to be produced in good order on each day of Exercise, and in such good order to be delivered up when required to the Commanding Officer, or such person or persons as shall under his Majesty's authority be commissioned to receive the same; And that every man be responsible for the care and safety of his Arms and Accoutrements, and be bound to repair and replace them when necessary at his own expence.

That each Man shall be subject to such Penalties, Rules and Regulations as shall be from time to time agreed upon by the Commanding Officer of the Troop.

O A T H

> I .... Do sincerely swear that I will be faithful and bear true Allegiance to His Majesty (King William, *deleted*; Queen Victoria, *interlined*) and I do swear that I will faithfully serve in the First Troop of Warwickshire Yeomanry according to the terms of the enrolment thereof.

	NAME	RESIDENCE	WHEN ENROLLED	WHEN RESIGNED
1	William Dilke	Maxstoke Castle	21 Jan 1822	dead [1837]
2	Welchman Whateley	Bennetts Hill, Birmingham	12 Jan 1831	
3	George Chetwynd	Grendon Hall	23 Jan 1834	
4	William Wilmot	Coventry	21 Apr 1834	
5	(Thos Smith	[Meriden]	left)	resigned
6	(Robert Brown	Coleshill	1797)	
7	(Thos Oldham	Leamington Priors	21 Sep 1794)	
8	Luke Pearman	Berkswell	Mar 1823	
9	Thos Osborn	Meriden	Mar 1830	
10	(Josh Clark	Fillongley	——	left)
11	John Jones	Hampton-in-Arden	Apr 1830	
12	Thos Ibbotson	Arley	Sep 1830	
13	Jos. Whitehouse	Hampton-in-Arden	3 Sep 1828	
14	(John Cooper	Coleshill	May 1833)	resigned 1840
15	Joseph Parker	Meriden	12 May 1815	

16	(Wm Harper	Meriden	Nov 1821)	
17	(Thos. Bull	Long Itchington	Mar 1827	left)
18	(John Shakespeare	Coventry	25 [??] 1824	left)
		[? MS worn]		
19	Thomas Ballard	Corley	30 Sep 1828	
20	(John Clark	Coleshill	Nov 1832	left)
21	William Townshend	Astley	Apr 1831	query 1828
22	John Sabin	Meriden	May 1834	
23	(William Davis	Keresley		left)
24	John Cross	Keresley		resigned 1840
25	Stephen Laidler	Meriden	Apr 1834	
26	Ephraim Todd	Packington	Sep 1814	left
27	(Robert Holloway	Yardley	. . . 1830)	left 1839
28	(John Whitehouse	Hampton [?]	Aug 1829)	resigned 20 Feb 1832
29	William Healley	Packington	Mar 1829	
30	William Bonaker	Meriden	Aug 1814	
31	(Charles Bromley	Coleshill	Aug 1830	left)
32	Thomas Eaves	Coleshill	6 Apr 1829	

Sheet 2

33	(Jos. Dodwell	Packington)		
34	George Smith	Packington	3 Mar 1830	
35	William Bunkidge	Packington	Apr 1827	
36	Henry Whittem	Meriden	Apr 1829	
37	Francis Bint	Meriden	Apr 1827	
38	(John Dutton	Packington		left)
39	Richard Smout	Packington	Apr 1833	
40	(Thomas Rogers	Coventry	Apr 1816)	died
41	(Henry Brown	Coventry		left)
42	(Edward Mayou	Packington	Apr 1825)	resigned
43	(William Day	Meriden)		left
44	John Birch	Meriden	Apr 1815	
45	Samuel Beaufoy	Meriden	Apr 1828	
46	(George Repton	Berkswell		dead)
47	(Frederick Robinson	Coventry	7 Oct 1834)	resigned 1839
48	(Wm Kinch his mark X	Coventry	29 Apr 1835	left)
49	(Thomas Price	Coventry	20 Jun 1835	left)
50	(William Proctor	Meriden	9 Apr 1935	left)
51	Isaac P. Evans	Griff	[10] May 1836	
52	(Joseph Gardner	Coventry	11 May 1836	left)

53	(Francis Peasmell	Leamington	11 May 1836	left)
54	(John Brown	Leamington	11 May 1836	left)
55	(John Archer Squiers	Leamington Priors)		13 names wanting
56	Thomas Handly	Kenilworth	March 1815	
57	(William Oldham	Leamington	— 1832	transferred)
58	(David Wakelin	Allesley	— 1809	left)
59	(Thomas Hopkins	Leamington	11 May 1836	left)
60	Edward Todd	Packington	May 1820	
61	(John Perry	Solihull		left)
62	Samuel Wakelin	Meriden	1809	
63	(John Burbidge	Coleshill	May 1808)	resigned in favour of his son 1839
64	Thomas Bloxsidge	Snowford	22 July 1833	
65	J. V. Walker	Meriden	May 1825	query 1822
66	Henry Carter Hopkins	Leamington	20 May 1836	left; transferred to troop
67	Daniel Barnes	Coventry	May 22, 1837	(resigned)
68	A. J. Payne	Coventry	Apr 1837	+1840, being about two years absent
69	John Pearson	Meriden	Aug 1837	
70	(Robert Hall	Coventry	Aug 1837	dead)
71	(John Knight	Leamington	Aug 1837	left)
72	(William Loade	Maxstock	Apr 1837	resigned 3 Oct 1841)
73	(John Archer Squiers	Leamington Priors	22 Jly 1833)	transferred to another troop, 1839
74	(Joseph Cross	Corley	12 Aug 1837	resigned 1840)
75	(Ben. Rhodes	Coventry	17 Jan 1838	dead)
76	Henry Thornley	Marston Hall	26 Feb 1838	
77	Eph^m Todd	Packington	21 Apr 1838	quere X
78	(Thomas Bull	Nuneaton	23 Apr 1838)	left 1840
79	(Samuel Compton	Exhall	23 Apr 1838)	resigned 1840
80	(William Drakeford	Exhall	23 Apr 1838)	left Mar 1840
81	John Lasselles	Bickenhill	23 Apr 1838	
82	Joseph Dodwell	Great Packington	20 May 1830	resigned in favour of his son 1839
83	Thomas Barnacle	Leamington	29 Apr 1838	left)
84	(John Burman	Leamington	23 Apr 1838	left)
85	(Samuel Bloxham	Leamington	23 Apr 1838	left)

86	Thomas X Shelton	Coventry	3 Apr 1838	resigned
87	(Charles Shewring	Coventry	21 May 1838	left)
88	(John Allwood	Leamington	18 Aug 1838	left)
89	(William Turner	Cubbington	18 Aug 1838	left)
90	(Thomas Janett	Attleborough	1 Mar 1839)	resigned 1844
91	(Benjamin Stratton	Griff	8 Mar 1839)	died 20 Nov 1846
92	(Samuel Nuttall	Griff	8 Mar 1839)	resigned 1 Mar 1847
93	(Charles Wilkinson	Coton	8 Mar 1839)	resigned 1842
94	Mathew Marks	Berkswell	8 Mar 1839	
95	(William Kelley	Berkswell	8 Mar 1839)	resigned 1843
96	(Charles Jefferies	Berkswell	8 Mar 1839)	resigned 1840
97	Samuel Taylor	Coton	8 Mar 1839	
98	(Josiah Allen	Coton	8 Mar 1839)	resigned 3 Feb 1847

Sheet 3

99	(Joseph Wilkinson	Coventry	1 Aug 1839)	resigned 1840
100	(John Townshend	Coventry	1 Aug 1839)	resigned 1839
101	(Thomas Clarke	Coventry	1 Aug 1839)	resigned 1840
102	Charles Keatley	Great Packington	1 Aug 1838	
103	Edward Mayou, junior	Great Packington	21 Aug 1839	
104	Thomas Burbidge	Coleshill	Jun 1840	
105	Thomas Oldham	Great Packington	Jun 1840	
106	David Trevor	Grey Friars Lane, Coventry	31 Aug 1840	
107	James Swinburn	Bickenhill	31 Aug 1840	
108	(Joseph Cleaver	Coventry	31 Aug 1840)	resigned 1842
109	(Charles [?*name* faded]	Coventry	4 Sep 1841)	resigned 1842
110	(John K [?*name* faded]	Coventry	4 Sep 1840)	
111	(Thomas Barrett	Coventry	19 Sep 1840)	
112	Thomas Proof	Bickinhill	16 Apr 1840	
113	Danl Gibbins	Bickenhill	20 Mar 1841	
114	William Brown	Coleshill	12 Mar 1842	
115	(William Wheeler	Packington	1 Mar 1843)	resigned 3 Mar 1847
116	John Oreton	Hampton	1 Mar 1843	
117	William Hard	Chilvers Coton	12 Mar 1843	

118	John Southill	Chilvers Coton	12 Mar 1843	
119	Henry Moore	Attleborough	12 Mar 1843	
120	Richard Hollick	Bedworth	20 Apr 1843	
121	Francis Freeman	Coton	23 Apr 1843	
122	Henry Williams	Leamington	1 May 1843	
123	(Stephen Britain	Berkswell	20 Apr 1844)	
124	John Smith	Astley	1 Mar 1844	
125	(William Baker	Attleborough	10 Apr 1844)	resigned 1 Nov 1846
126	(Edward Lowe	Hampton	25 May 1843)	died 30 Oct 1846
127	William Whittaker	Hampton	1 May 1844	
128	William Russell	Meriden	28 Mar 1846	
129	John Johnson [?]	Bickenhill	May 1847	
130	John Murcott	Offchurch	Mar 1847	
131	Thomas Whitehouse	Offchurch	Mar 1847	
132	Henry Goffe	Offchurch	Mar 1847	
133	Edward Inett	Fillongley	Mar 1847	
134	Andrew Britain	Berkswell	Apr 1848	
135	Mark Newton	Meriden	Apr 1848	
136	Samuel Parker	Exhall	Mar 1847	
137	Edward Bint	Meriden	Mar 1847	
138	Thomas Blissell	Hampton	Mar 1847	
139	Wm Humphrey Harper	Meriden	Mar 1847	
140	William Rose	Offchurch	Mar 1847	

Sheet 4

141	Edward Atkins	Coventry	9 Aug 1853
142	John Brooke	Coventry	9 Aug 1853
143	William Ball	Bickenhill	27 Sep 1854
144	Francis Britain	Berkswell	27 Sep 1854

[*blank line; entries 145 onwards in a new, clear hand, presumably Capt. A .E. Pretyman's*]

145	Captain Pretyman, A. C.	Nuneaton	May 1863
146	Lieut Somerville, Hon. H.	Leamington	
147	Cornet Woodcock, George	Coventry	

148	(Q'master Pearson, John	Meriden)	signed above ACP	
149	(Sergeant-Major Brown, Robert	Coleshill)	signed above ACP	
150	(Sergeant Smith, George	Packington)	signed above ACP	
151	Sergeant East, Thomas	Coventry	Oct 1849	dead ACP
152	Sergeant Sharpe, Henry	Packington	Apr 1857	
153	Sergeant Bint, Edward	Meriden	Aug 1847	
154	Corporal Shakespeare, William	Hampton	Apr 1857	
155	Corporal Whittem, Albert	Meriden	Apr 1857	
156	Trumpeter Cox, John	Leamington	May 1857	
157	Private Arnold, John	Meriden	Apr 1860	
158	Private (Barnes, Daniel	Coventry)	signed above ACP	
159	Private Barnes, Riley	ditto	Apr 1863	resigned ACP
160	Private Ball, William	Bickenhill	Sep 1854	
161	(Band, Blandford, Wm	Leamington)		left 1865, ACP
162	Private Brown, David	Coventry		
163	Private Brown, Henry	Coventry	Apr 1864	
164	Private Brittain, Francis	Berkswell	Sep 1854	
165	Private Brettle, Thomas	Hampton	Apr 1850	
166	Private Butler, Arthur	Coventry	Apr 1864	
167	Private Crier, Thomas	Coomb	Apr 1864	resigned 1867 ACP
168	Private Dunn, Thomas	Coventry		Sept., 1865 ACP
169	Private Dutton, Thomas	Bickenhill		
170	Private Gilbert, William	Meriden	Apr 1858	
171	Private Harper, Edward	Meriden	April, 1860	
172	Private Hunt, John	Meriden		
173	Private Ibbotson, William	Arley	Apr 1864	
174	Private Johnson, Jos.	Bickenhill	Apr 1864	
175	Farrier Jones, John	Hampton		Sep 1865, ACP
176	Farrier Keatley, Chas	Packington	Apr 1838	
177	Private Kemp, George	Bickenhill	Apr 1864	
178	(Cpl Laidler, Stephen	Berkswell)	signed above	
179	Private Lee, Arthur	Meriden	May 1862	
180	Private Lovett, Thos	Coventry	Sep 1863	

181	Private Oldham, Henry	Packington	Apr 1864	
182	Private Parker, James	Meriden	Apr 1861	
183	Private Riley, Luke	Packington	Apr 1862	
184	Private Salt, Abraham	Coventry	Apr 1861	
185	Private Shakespeare, Thomas	Barston	Apr 1857	
186	Corporal Steedman, Jos	Meriden	Apr 1860	
187	Private Smith, Henry	(Coomb) Brinklow		
188	(Private Todd, Ephraim	Bickenhill)	Signed above ACP	
189	Private Thompson, John	Birmingham		
190	Private Weetman, Tom	Ansley	Apr 1864	Resigned 1867 ACP
191	Private Weetman, Jos.	Ansley	Apr 1864	Resigned 1866 ACP
192	Private Wilday, Wm	Bedworth	Apr 1853	
193	Private Whitehouse, Wm	Hampton	Apr 1853	

Sheet 5

194	Private Freeman, Benjamin	Allesley	Apr 1865
195	Private Pebiady, Alfred	Allesley	Apr 1865
196	Private Ibbetson, Wm	Arley	Apr 1864
197	Private Torbitt, Joseph	Ansley	Mar 1865
198	Private Robottom, Jos.	Hartshill	Mar 1865
199	Private Wilkinson, Wm	Meriden	Apr 1865
200	Band Warden, Alfred	Leamington	Apr 1865
201	Private Buckler, Thos	Chapel End, Nuneaton	19 Mar 1867
202	Private King, John	Olton, Solihull	7 May 1867
203	Private Hughes, Thos	Olton, Solihull	7 May 1867
204	Private Taylor, William	Astley, Nuneaton	7 May 1867
205	Private Gilbert, Charles	Packington	7 May 1867
206	Private Bromwich, Jos.	Olton, Solihull	7 May 1867
207	Private West, John	Astley, Nuneaton	7 May 1867
208	Private Bullock, Henry	Arbury, Nuneaton	7 May 1867
209	Private Bromwich, John	Arbury, Nuneaton	7 May 1867
210	[*Blank*]	Arbury, Nuneaton	7 May 1867
211	[*tear*]atford, William	Arbury, Nuneaton	7 May 1867
212	Private Morton, Thos	Arbury, Nuneaton	7 May 1867

213	Private Riley, Alfred	Arbury, Nuneaton	
214	[Lieut Al]ston, William Charles	Elmdon Hall, Birmingham	23 Aug 1865
215	Private Dexter, Thomas	Coventry	Apr 1868
216	Private Jephcott, Isaac	Ansley	May 1868

THE ROLL OF THE SECOND TROOP OF THE WARWICKSHIRE YEOMANRY *c.* 1836–1898

Warwickshire Yeomanry Museum, Warwick
Reproduced by permission of the Trustees

Articles of Enrolment of the Second Troop of Yeomanry Cavalry for the County of Warwick

We whose Names are hereunto subscribed in pursuance of an Act of Parliament passed in the Forty second year of his Majesty King George the Third entitled 'An Act to enable His Majesty to avail Himself of the Offers of certain Yeomanry and Volunteer Corps to continue their Services' do voluntarily enrol ourselves in the Corps of Cavalry called the Yeomanry of the County of Warwick formed for the Internal Defence and Security of the Kingdom, on the following Conditions

1 The Officers to receive Commissions from his Majesty or from the Lord Lieutenant of the County, or others who may be especially authorized by his Majesty for that purpose.

2 The Corps to be subject to be embodied in case of Invasion, or an appearance thereof, or in case of Rebellion or Insurrection and to be Marched to any part of the Kingdom of Great Britain and to be subject to be called upon for the suppression of Riots or Tumults within the County of Warwick or any adjoining County.

3 To receive no pay, unless when embodied or called out, but to attend, mounted on a Serviceable Gelding or Mare, to be approved by the Commanding Officer of the Troop, for the purpose of exercise at such times and places as shall be fixed by such Commanding officer.

4 In all cases when Embodied or called out on Service, to receive pay as allowed by Government and to be subject to Military Discipline as the rest of his Majesty's regular and Militia Forces.

5 Such Articles as are furnished by Government, and shall be

allowed to each Man to be produced in good order on each day of exercise and in such good order to be delivered up when required to the Commanding Officer, or such person or persons as shall, under his Majesty's authority be commissioned to receive the same: And that every Man be responsible for the care and safety of his Arms and Accoutrements and be bound to repair and replace them, if necessary, at his own expence.

6   That each Man shall be subject to such Penalties, Rules and Regulations as shall be from time to time agreed upon by the Commanding Officer of the Troop.

OATH

I .... Do sincerely swear that I will be faithful and bear true Allegiance to His Majesty King William, and I do swear that I will faithfully serve in the second Troop of the Warwickshire Yeomanry according to the Terms of the Enrolment thereof.

	NAME	RESIDENCE	WHEN ENROLLED	WHEN RESIGNED
217	Samuel Harrison	Tanworth	16 Jan 1834	
218	William [Pear?]man	Birmingham	6 Mar 1834	
219	David Vincent	Birmingham	6 Mar 1834	
220	Humphrey Welch	Aston	6 Mar 1834	
221	John Ingerthorp	Solihull	7 Jly 1834	
222	William Taylor	Birmingham	3 Dec 1834	
223	William Beech	Birmingham	3 Dec 1834	
224	William Robinson	Birmingham	3 Dec 1834	
225	[John ?] Marshall	Birmingham	21 Jan 1835	
226	Edward York	Birmingham	15 Apr 1835	
227	Joseph Smith	Birmingham	16 Apr 1835	
228	Edward Bayles	Lapworth	14 Apr 1836	
229	John Wood	Hockley	14 Apr 1836	
230	Thomas Bradbury	Tanworth	21 Apr 1836	
231	James Miller	Hockley	21 Apr 1836	
232	John Crockett	Elmdon	6 May 1836	
233	Thomas Jay	Birmingham	8 May 1836	

234	Ja^s Robinson	Birmingham	[4 Jun?], 1836
235	John Starkey	Birmingham	4 Jun 1836
236	Thomas Webb	Birmingham	7 Jan 1837
237	G. Ed [???]	Birmingham	26 May 1837
238	John Kid	Lapworth	2 Aug 1837

Sheet 2

239	John Cartland	Birmingham	22 Jly 1837
240	William Henry Iliffe	Birmingham	28 Oct 1837
241	G. L. Walker	Birmingham	28 Oct 1837
242	John Davis	Birmingham	30 Oct 1837
243	Major Brindley	Birmingham	21 May 1838
244	William Young	Birmingham	21 May 1838
245	Joseph Paget	Tanworth	25 May 1838
246	Thos. Court	Shrewley	25 May 1838
247	William Draper	Claverdon	25 May 1838
248	George Hickin	Claverdon	25 May 1838
249	Barnabas Cheshire	Beaudesert	25 May 1838
250	James Firth	Handsworth	25 Jly 1838
251	Edward Moore	Handsworth	25 Jly 1838
252	William Foster	Birmingham Heath	25 Jly 1838
253	Edward Coleman	Birmingham	11 Oct 1838
254	Thos Bateman	....	Sep 1835
255	Thos Canning	Lapworth	16 Dec 1835
256	Richd Cotterrell	Lapworth	16 Sep 1835
257	Ja^s Lancaster	....	5 May 1834
258	Thos Rollason	Birmingham	Sept 1831
259	Saml Smith	Tanworth	12 Dec 1833
260	H. Tailby	....	25 Jly 1838
261	[William?] Wilkes	Tanworth	[25?] Jly 1838
262	Robt Belcher	....	Sep 1831
263	Jos^h Harbidge	....	Sep 1831
264	Adam Jowat	Handsworth	24 Nov 1838
265	George Beilby	Hockley	22 May 1839
266	Benjamin Whelldon	Tanworth	28 Jun 1839
267	Wm Chadshaw [*sic*]	Birmingham	28 Jun 1839
268	John Yates	Washwood	28 Jun 1839
269	Jo^s Mills	Alcester	28 Jun 1839
270	Thos Hopkins	Henley-in-Arden	28 Jun 1839
271	William Woodward	Packwood	28 Jun 1839
272	Joseph Allcock	Packwood	28 Jun 1839

273	Edwd Hayes	Knowle	28 Jun 1839
274	Thos Appelbee	Henley[-in-]Arden	28 Jun 1839
275	Edmund Allen	Residence Basall	15 Aug 1839
276	William Hilditch	Tanworth	15 Aug 1839

Sheet 3

277	Richard J. Heath	Balsall	22 Aug 1839
278	H.A. Dauncey	Birmingham	19 Sep 1839
279	J. Booth	Birmingham	19 Sep 1839
280	J. Salt	Tanworth	19 Sep 1839
281	E. S. Haycock	Birmingham	23 Dec 1839
282	W. H. Jones	Birmingham	23 Dec 1839
283	C. J. Mainstone	Birmingham	4 Jan 1840
284	John Weaver	Birmingham	16 Mar 1840
285	Thomas Dews Tolly	Birmingham	9 Mar 1840
286	William Burt	Birmingham	26 Sep 1840
287	Henry H[arvey?]	Birmingham	29 Sep 1840
*288	Thomas Bluck	Wroxall	[15 Sep] 1840
*289a	Thomas Turner	Birmingham	11 Mar 1840
**289b	Joseph Pearman	Wroxall	11 Mar 1840
290	John Weldon	Birmingham	10 Dec 1840
291	William Browne	Birmingham	4 Mar 1841
**292	William Riley	Balsall	25 Feb 1841
**293	George Coppage	Henley-in-Arden	15 May 1841
**294	Richard Harrison	Henley-in-Arden	15 May 1841
**295	Edwin Reeves	Birmingham	15 May 1841
**296	Saml Walker	Birmingham	8 Sep 1841
**297	David Knight	Birmingham	9 Sep 1841
**298	Joseph Ball	Hockley	9 Sep 1841
**299	William Mander	Beaudesert	9 Sep 1841
**300	Gregory Hickman Packer	Hockley	9 Sep 1841
*301	Edwin Hopkins	Henley-in-Arden	9 Sep 1841
**302	Samuel M. Bradbury	Birmingham	17 Mar 1842
303	William Turbeyfield	Birmingham	15 Feb 1842
304	Samuel Lucas	Tanworth	2 May 1842
305	Francis Stafford	Solihull	2 May 1842
306	Henry Latham	Solihull	2 May 1842
307	Horatio Powell	Birmingham	17 Mar 1842
308	Thomas Godfrey	Henley-in-Arden	15 May 1846 [sic]
309	Joseph Thurman	Birmingham	22 Oct 1842
310	Edwd. B. Baldwin	Birmingham	3 Nov 1842

| 311 | John Kemp | Birmingham | 26 Jly 1843 |
| 312 | John Izod | Tanworth | 15 May 1846 |

Sheet 4

313	Henry Tilsley	Lapworth	28 Apr 1845	
314	William Yeomans	Ullenhall	22 May 1844	
315	Joseph Wilton	76 Broad St, Islington, Birmingham	22 May 1844	
**316	William Hemming	Henley-In-Arden	22 May 1844	
**317	Thomas Riley	Balsall	22 May 1844	
*318	Chas Armstrong	Birmingham	9 May 1844	
319	Isaac Taylor	Wroxhall	11 Mar 1845	
320	George Reaves	Berkswell	11 Mar 1845	
321	Chandos Wren Hoskyns	Wroxhall	9 May 1845	
322	Thomas Tibbetts Jennaway	Henley-in-Arden	9 May 1845	
323	James Baldwin	Lapworth	9 May 1845	
324	William Daniel Hands	Birmingham	15 May 1846	
325	Joseph Hawkes	Wootton Wawen	16 May 1846	
326	John Gibbs	Edstone	16 May 1846	
327	Thomas Draper	Claverdon	20 May 1846	
328	Edwd. Jorden	Bearley	20 May 1846	
329	Henry Hancox	Aston Row Town Birm. [?]	26 May 1841	
330	Thomas Arblaster	Hockley Heath	24 May 1843	
331	Henry Meredith	Henley-in-Arden	15 May 1848	
332	John Whateley	Redditch	24 May1843	
333	John Gibbs	Edstone	16 May 1846	signed 7 lines above
334	John Greves	Chadshunt	15 May 1848	
335	Thomas Taylor	Wolverton	15 May 1848	
336	Joseph Shakespear	Preston Baggot	15 May 1848	
337	Charles Silvester	Cleeve Prior-Bidford	15 May 1848	
338	William Wyatt	Crabs Cross-Redditch	15 May 1848	
339	John Wilson	Edstone	15 May 1848	
340	Edward Parker	Binton	15 May 1848	
341	Charles Ford	Inkberrow	15 May 1848	
342	William Ford	Inkberrow	15 May 1848	

343	Joseph Wood	Hockley Heath	15 May 1848
344	John Lee	Claverdon	15 May 1848
345	Richard Nash	Inkberrow	15 May 1848
346	[Augustine] Bayliss	Inkberrow	15 May 1848
347	John Taylor	Tanworth	24 Mar 1849
348	John Hawkes	Henley-in-Arden	15 May 1848
349	George Mann	Stratford-on-Avon	14 May 1850
350	William Parish	Birmingham	15 May 1848

Sheet 5

351	Robert Reid	Alveston	23 Jly 1847
352	Edward Raleigh King	Chadshunt	21 Dec 1848
353	John Tom Clarke	Warwick	21 Dec 1848
354	Thomas Elwin Standish	Warwick	21 Dec 1848
355	Joseph Brearley	Cookhill, Inkberrow	2 May 1849
356	Edward Larkings	Langley	21 Aug 1849
357	William Whittington	Claverdon	3 Oct 1849
358	George Ford	Hanbury	3 Oct 1849
359	William Wincott	Alveston	3 Oct 1849
360	Joseph Robinson	Birmingham	3 Oct 1849
361	Thomas Ivens	Lour [sic] Norton	14 May 1850
362	John Mansell	Preston	26 May 1852
363	George Bloomer	Henley-in-Arden	25 May 1852
364	Thomas Hood	Solihull	25 May 1852
365	Charles Jackson	Tanworth	25 May 1852
366	William Parker	Badsey	25 May 1852
367	Charles Harding	Birmingham	25 May 1852
368	George Clark	Wootton Wawen	25 May 1852
369	Thomas Chinn	Knowle	19 Jun 1852
370	William Cotterell	Balsall	19 Jun 1852
371	Joseph Cotterell	Balsall	19 Jun 1852
372	Edward Mander	Beaudesert	29 Jun 1852
373	John Iliffe	Birmingham	30 Jun 1852
374	John Harvey	Birmingham	30 Jun 1852
375	John James Kimbell	Knowle	21 Sep 1852
376	George Hodges	Lapworth	14 May 1853
377	John Meads	Eatington	14 May 1853
378	Frederick Buller	Stratford-on-Avon	14 May 1853
379	William Baylis	Stratford-on-Avon	14 May 1853
380	Thomas Edwards	Stratford-on-Avon	14 May 1853
381	Thomas Hawkes	Haselor	1 Jun 1854

382	Joseph Richards	Inkberrow	14 May 1853
383	Geoffrey Stafford	Solihull	14 May 1853
384	Sam\. Edkins	Henley-in-Arden	14 May 1853
385	Will\. Cooke	Warwick	14 May 1853
386	Edward Kite	Claverdon	————
387	Henry Pratt	Claverdon	17 May 1855
388	George Talliss	Snitterfield	17 May 1855

Sheet 6

389	Philip Wakeham Martin	Leamington	3 Oct 1855	
390	Joseph Ball	Packwood Hall	17 May 1855	
391	Josiah Bott	Tanworth	17 May 1855	
392	Thomas Rainbow	Tanworth	17 May 1855	
393	Joseph Taylor	Tanworth	17 May 1855	
394	George Hickin	Lapworth	17 May 1855	
395	David Banister	Solihull	17 May 1855	
396	John Tite	Beaudesert	17 May 1855	
397	Job Bellamy	Lapworth	17 May 1855	
398	Michael Brookes	Solihull		
399	Christopher Farr			
400	Darwin Galton	Edstone	21 May 1855	Cornet in 3d Troop, 2 Apr 1838; Captain 2nd Troop, 8 Aug 1845
401	John Sabin	Henley-in-Arden	21 May 1855	Joined Troop 1 Apr 1852
402	Henry Charles Palmer	Lighthorne	8 Oct 1855	
403	Tom Jeffcoat	Nuthurst	8 Oct 1855	
404	John Chesshire	Lapworth	8 Oct 1855	
405	Matthew Marlow Hinks	Knowle	8 Oct 1855	
406	Thomas Jackson	Rowington	15 Dec 1855	
407	W. S. Bott	Ullenhall	2 May 1856	
408	J. W. Colledge	Ullenhall	2 May 1856	
409	Charles Richards	Solihull	26 May 1858	
410	William Hickin	Lapworth	28 May 1858	
411	George Shrimpton	Feckenham	26 May 1858	
412	Samuel Fullard	Packwood	28 May 1858	
413	Thomas Ball	Packwood	28 May 1858	
414	John Ball	Nuthurst	16 Sep 1859	
415	William Taylor	Tanworth	26 Sep1861	

416	Edwin Proctor	Handsworth	23 Oct 1861
417	George Billing	Packwood	23 Oct 1861
418	Thomas Chesshire	Hockley	23 Oct 1861
419	John P[aston?]	Tanworth	23 Oct 1861
420	John Neason	Tanworth	23 Oct 1861

Sheet 7

421	William Ball	Lapworth	23 Oct 1861	
422	John Dowdeswell	Nuthurst	23 Oct 1861	resigned 27 Mar 1871
423	William Hy. Coppage	Henley-in-Arden	23 Oct 1861	
424	Benjamin Turner	Tanworth	23 Oct 1861	
425	Henry Johns	Henley-in-Arden	23 Oct 1861	
426	Francis Badger	Bearley	23 Oct 1861	
427	William F[idesmere?]	Solihull	23 Oct 1861	
428	G. F. Muntz	Umberslade	11 Dec 1861	
429	C. [Young?]	Knowl	11 Dec 1863	
430	W. J. Sheldon	Earlswood	————	
431	C. R. Green	Claverdon	1867	resigned 25 Feb 1884
432	T. W. Whitehouse	Solihull	1870	deceased 28 Aug 1877
433	Insull Burman	Olton	1870	
434	W. S. Fulford	Acocks Green	1871	resigned 16 Jun 1876
435	E. Tallis	Packwood		resigned 29 Mar 1880
436	C. Chambers	Hockley Heath		resigned 1 Apr 1880
437	W. T. Middleton	Claverdon		resigned 27 Feb 1884
438	James Whittindale	Hampton-in-Arden		1868 resigned 1875
439	John Edwd. Pitt	————		resigned 25 Apr 1863
440	Joseph Fullard	Manor Farm, Packwood	1867	resigned 1 Apr 1875
441	William Vernon	Lapworth	1869	resigned 3 May 1881
442	J. S. Reeve	Elmdon	1871	resigned 1 Apr 1878

443	E. G. Peters	Birmingham	1873	resigned 1 Apr 1878
444	H. P. Boughton	Erdington	1873	resigned 1873
445	Thomas Henry Barns	Copt Heath	1873	resigned 16 Apr 1877
446	W. C. Alston	Elmdon Hall	1872	
447	John Hetherington	Edstone		resigned Nov 1887
448	Thos King	Rowington		
449	John Oakley	Knowle	1873	resigned April 1876
450	Edmund Francis	Elmdon Hall	1873	
451	Thos King	Solihull	1871	resigned 24 Apr 1881
452	E. H. Brown	Birmingham	1873	deserted 1 Apr 1876

Sheet 8

453	Arthur A. Ball	Packwood	1874	resigned 1 Apr 1879
454	John Ball	Nuthurst	1874	resigned 1 Apr 1880
455	Clement Butler	Elmdon	1874	resigned 1 Apr 1877
456	Frederick Mettell	Elmdon	1874	[resigned 1 Apr 1876, *deleted*]
457	W . J. Clements	Birmingham	1871	resigned 20 Mar 1877
458	James Jennings	Birmingham	1873	resigned 4 Jly 1878
459	Wm Thorp Monsley	Shirley	1873	resigned 10 Sep 1876
460	William Henry Bryan	Snitterfield	1874	
461	John Gray	Sutton Coldfield	1874	resigned 1 Apr 1878
462	Gilbert H. C. Leigh	Stonleigh Abbey	1874	promoted Captain 5th Troop, 1877
463	Walter Goodswell Clark	14 Temple Street Chambers, [Birmingham]	1874	resigned May 1875

464	Frank C. Hornby	Eastcote	1875	resigned 16 Jan 1880
465	George Thompson	Shirley	1875	resigned 1878
466	Saml. Benj. Barnes	Olton	1875	resigned
467	Thomas Ward	Handsworth	1875	
468	Arthur Smith	Elmdon	1875	resigned 1 Jan 1877
**469	George Gaywood	Elmdon	1873	resigned 27 Feb 1880
*470	[John?] Potter	Hampton-in-Arden		resigned 1 Apr 1876
471	John Buckler	46 Lancaster St Birmingham	26 Jly 1875	resigned 27 Jan 1880
472	Walter Billing	Hockley Heath	27 Oct 1875	resigned 1 Apr 1879
473	Frank Soulby	Turl Street, Oxford	6 Jan 1876	resigned 1 Apr 1879
474	Edwin Henry Wilson	Solihull	10 Jan 1876	resigned 1 Apr 1878
*475	—— Parker	——————	7 Feb 1876	[*pencil*]
476	Henry Heath	Knowle	9 Feb 1876	resigned 14 Apr 1881
477	Archibald M. McInnes	42 Bath Row, Birmingham	14 Feb 1876	resigned by special permission 30 Jun 1876
478	Ernest Orford	Solihull	14 Feb 1876	resigned 4 Feb 1878
479	Russell Orford	Solihull	14 Feb 1876	resigned 4 Feb1878
480	William Beaufoy	Knowle	24 Feb 1878	resigned 18 Feb 1880

Sheet 9

481	Edward Randel	Selly Oak	24 Feb 1876	resigned 1 Apr 1878
482	Edward Avery	Bentley Heath	29 Feb 1876	resigned 1 Apr 1878
483	John Brookes	Shirley	29 Feb 1876	resigned 1 Apr 1879
484	Alfred Allen	Shirley	25 Mar 1876	resigned 1 Apr 1879

485	William Terry	Sparkbrook	27 Mar1876	resigned 14 Apr 1881
486	George Henry Hooker	Handsworth	1 May 1876	resigned 8 Mar 1878
487	Heber Howard	Yardley	12 Jly 1876	resigned 16 Jan 1880
488	Joseph Greenway	Moseley	12 Jly 1876	deserted
489	John Findon	Aston	12 Jly 1876	resigned 12 May 1880
490	[F?] Ballard	Sutton	14 Jly1876	resigned 1 Apr 1878 by order Inspector General
491	F. Gregg	Birmingham	15 Jly, 1876	
492	Fredk J. [Levy?]	Birmingham	3 Nov 1876	resigned 3 Feb 1880
493	Aug. A. Fridlander	Birmingham	3 Nov 1876	resigned 26 Mar 1881
494	John Gage	Elmdon Heath, Solihull	27 Nov 1876	Drill Instructor
**495	[William Grant	Henley-in-Arden]	[*Entry deleted*]	
496	Frederick H. Fiddian	Birmingham	15 Jan 1877	resigned 9 Apr 1882
497	Joseph Judge Skinner	Birmingham	15 Jan 1877	deserted
498	Arthur Turner	Birmingham	23 Jan 1877	resigned 9 Apr 1882
499	George Smith	Birmingham	25 Jan1877	resigned 5 Mar1880
500	Charles P. Pollock	Birmingham	1 Feb 1877	resigned 7 Mar1885
501	George Henry Johnson	Birmingham	1 Feb 1877	resigned 15 May 1881
502	Felix Jones	Birmingham	27 Mar 1877	resigned 1 May 1880
503	Henry James Bailey	Birmingham	26 Apr 1877	resigned 16 Feb 1880
504	Edwin Gill	Birmingham	5 May 1877	resigned 15 Apr 1882
505	Alfred Hathaway	Birmingham	24 Jly 1877	resigned 15 Apr 1882
506	Alfred Hawkes	Birmingham	24 Jly 1877	resigned 1 Dec 1880
507	William Henry Izon	Birmingham	24 Jly 1877	deceased

508	John Francis Dabbs	Birmingham	3 Jan 1878	resigned 1 Dec 1880
509	John Hall Gibbons	Birmingham	3 Jan 1878	resigned 9 May 1881
510	William Izon	Packwood	6 Feb 1878	resigned 16 Feb 1880
511	Charles Joseph Fletcher	Birmingham	5 Mar 1878	resigned 10 May 1881
512	Geo. Stanley Purden	Birmingham	26 Mar 1878	resigned 18 Jly 1890
513	[*Bottom of sheet trimmed and one name lost*]			

Sheet 10

514	John Meynell Hunt	Birmingham	1 Apr 1878	
515	[V. H.?] G. Page	Birmingham	18 Nov 1878	resigned 5 Apr 1882
516	[F. C.?] Dicke	Birmingham	18 Nov 1878	resigned 9 Apr 1882 deceased 8 Jun 1890
517	W. F. Field	Birmingham	18 Nov 1878	[deceased 13 Apr 1883 *deleted*]
518	Chas W. Garbett	Birmingham	18 Nov 1878	resigned 1 May 1882
519	Albert Anthony	Birmingham	14 Feb 1879	resigned 1 May 1882
520	Clement S. Jones	Birmingham	14 Feb 1879	deserted 1 May 1882
521	William G. Lewis	Birmingham	27 Mar 1879	resigned 1 May 1882
522	Thomas Johnston	Birmingham	30 May 1879	
523	William Green	Birmingham	9 Jly 1879	resigned
524	A. O. Hutchins	Birmingham	4 Dec 1879	deserted
525	G. Brookes	Luscombe, Snitterfield	16 Feb 1880	resigned 12 Feb 1885
526	J. Pearman	The Quinton, Birmingham	16 Feb 1880	resigned 25 Feb 1883
527	W. J. Day	Birmingham	5 Mar 1880	
528	Edw. Haye	Birmingham	24 Mar 1880	resigned 25 Feb 1883
529	J. Thurston	Birmingham	18 Aug, 1880	rcsigned 11 Aug 1885

530	J. C. Gillibrand	————————	9 May 1881	resigned 27 Jun 1884
531	J. Whitby	Birmingham	12 Apr 1881	resigned 22 Mar 1886
532	J. Morris	Birmingham	26 Jly 1881	deserted 10 Oct 1885
533	J. Smith	Birmingham	1 Aug 1881	deserted 8 Aug 1882
534	E. J. Abbott	Handsworth	6 Aug 1881	resigned 7 Jan 1887
535	Fred. F. Flinn	Handsworth	6 Aug 1881	resigned 11 Aug 1884
536	H. Scott Smith	Handsworth	7 Oct 1881	enrollment cancelled
537	A. C. Bishop	Aston	7 Oct 1881	resigned 1 Nov 1884
538	[A?] C. Chandler	Wylde Green	26 Nov 1881	resigned 12 Apr 1883
539	J. Boston	Acocks Green	26 Nov 1881	deserted 8 Aug 1882
541	Edward Kirkham	Hawkwell Hall, Great Barr	28 Nov 1881	resigned 7 Aug 1884
542	Thos Arthur Slie	Aston	10 Dec 1881	resigned 1 Aug 1889
543	John G [ays?]	Elmdon Heath, Birmingham	29 Nov 1881	resigned 18 May 18[*blot*]
544	Jabez Sarsons	Small Heath	4 Jan 1882	resigned 24 May 1887
545	Walter T. Fawdry	Birmingham	27 Feb 1882	resigned 3 Mar 1885
546	T. J. Boyle	Henley-in-Arden	27 Feb 1882	resigned 14 Mar 1885
547	C. W. Mayou	Henley-in-Arden	27 Feb 1882	deserted 25 Jan 1885
548	Frank Dugdale	Wroxall Abbey	Oct 1880	O. C. Regiment Dec 1911
549	John Tookey	Birmingham	3 Apr 1882	
550	F. Ford Pinchbeck	Birmingham	[Apr *deleted*] 8 Aug 1882	deceased 17 Jly 1887
551	Thos Johnson	Dudley	8 Aug 1882	resigned 21 Mar 1889
552	H.A. Gibbs	Birmingham	25 Aug 1882	resigned 19 Nov 1883

Sheet 11

553	Arthur W. Marlow	Handsworth	2 Sep 1882	resigned 2 Sep 1885
554	Frank Brown	Birmingham	6 Sep 1882	resigned 13 Apr 1886
555	Mostyn Jones	Birmingham	12 Jan 1883	resigned 13 May 1889
556	Alfred Harris	Aston	14 Feb 1883	resigned
557	Edward M. Shaw	Birmingham	17 Feb 1883	resigned 6 Mar 1886
558	Robert [Bergin ?]	Birmingham	[Apr *deleted*] 13 Jan 1883	resigned 13 Apr 1886
559	Thomas E. Williams	Birmingham	1 Jan 1883	
560	John Harry Mills	Birmingham	5 Mar 1883	resigned
561	Lewis Wm Goold	Birmingham	11 Aug 1883	
562	Charles Tonks Bigford	Birmingham	9 Oct 1883	resigned 31 Mar 1887
563	William Francis Morris	Birmingham	10 Nov 1883	resigned Aug 1887
564	Ch. W. Neill	Birmingham	12 Nov 1883	resigned 20 Apr 1886
565	Ch. Danvers	Stechford	21 Dec 1883	resigned 3 Feb 1887
566	C. W. A. Foxwell	Birmingham	10 Jan 1884	resigned
567	G. S. Kelsey	Birmingham	10 Jan 1884	resigned 10 Jan 1887
568	Walter Thomas	Birmingham	17 Jan 1884	resigned 28 May 1887
569	R.M. Phipps	Lapworth T [*sic*]	17 Jan 1884	resigned 26 Jan 1886
570	P. Bans	Birmingham	19 Jan 1884	resigned 7 Nov 1885
571	Jno. Deeley Jr	Ward End, Birmingham	21 Jan 1884	resigned 16 Apr 1887
572	Henry Mitchell, junior	Cape Hill, Smethwick	31 May 1884	resigned 21 Apr 1888
573	J. Samuel Allen	Birmingham	8 Apr 1884	resigned 11 Feb 1885
574	W. H. Foxwell	Birmingham	22 May 1884	
575	N. H. Cattell	Birmingham	28 Jly 1884	resigned
576	J. C. Bartley	Birmingham	11 Feb 1885	resigned 5 Apr 1888

577	W. Rogers	Acocks Green	21 Feb 1885	resigned 24 Sep 1887
578	G. J. Evans	Erdington	[Feb *deleted*] 3 Mar 1885	resigned 15 May 1886
579	T. Styles	Birmingham	3 Mar 1885	resigned
580	J. A. Harrison	Aston House, Birm.	28 Jly 1885	resigned Aug 1887
581	Ernest W. Jones	Saltley, Birm.	28 Jly 1885	resigned 6 Apr 1889
582	Thomas Willmot	Birmingham	28 Jly 1885	resigned 21 Mar 1889
583	J. H. Gwyther	Birmingham	2 Oct 1885	deceased 12 Nov 1886
584	A. Thwaites	Birmingham	13 Oct 1885	resigned 14 May 1889
585	H. Spencer Smallman	Birmingham	2 Nov 1885	resigned 26 Jan 1889
586	Chas. A. Webster	Birmingham	24 Dec 1885	resigned 24 May 1889
587	Edward H. Guest	West Bromwich	18 Jan 1886	resigned Aug 1887
588	James Goffe	Birmingham	28 Jan 1886	resigned 28 Feb 1889
589	Angel Rose	Birmingham	9 Feb 1886	
590	J. Gray Styles	Birmingham	9 Feb 1886	
591	H. Turner	Birmingham	22 Feb 1886	resigned
592	K. James	Birmingham	16 Mar 1886	resigned
593	Chas F. Green	Birmingham	18 Jun 1886	resigned
594	Fred Griffiths	Birmingham	18 Jun 1886	resigned 8 Apr 1891
595	Wm Cooper	West Bromwich	9 Sep 1886	resigned 31 Mar 1888

Sheet 12

596	A. S. Neill [?]	West Bromwich	9 Sep 1886	resigned 8 May 1889
597	C. A. Smith	West Bromwich	11 Sep 1886	resigned 3 Mar 1888
598	Charles Larkins	Birmingham	11 Dec 1886	resigned 2 Mar 1889
599	Walter Jennings	Moseley	11 Dec 1886	resigned 13 May 1889

600	Thomas Vincent	Birmingham		resigned
601	Percy P. Burt	Birmingham	14 Feb 1887	resigned 27 Mar 1889
602	Edward Davenport	Birmingham	5 Mar 1887	resigned 27 Apr 1889
603	Baron J. Davenport	Birmingham	5 Mar 1887	resigned 13 Apr 1891
604	A. Harris	Birmingham	15 Mar 1887	resigned 27 Apr 1889
605	James A. Richards	Birmingham	9 Dec 1887	resigned 18 Mar 1893
606	M. Taylor	Birmingham	20 Feb 1888	resigned
607	W. Brocklebank	Birmingham	27 Feb 1888	resigned
608	J. H. Mills	Birmingham	13 Mar 1888	resigned 17 Apr 1892
609	W. Goff	Birmingham	22 Mar 1888	resigned
610	Frank [?J.] Walter	Birmingham	22 Mar 1888	resigned
611	Albert Ward	Birmingham	29 Mar 1888	resigned
*612	[Richard?] Davis	Birmingham	27 Apr 1888	resigned
613	F. H. Jenkins	Olton	20 Jun 1888	resigned
614	J. E. Garbett	[B, deleted] Solihull	20 Jun 1888	dismissed the Regiment
615	Geo. Norris Jnr	Birmingham	21 Jun 1888	resigned
616	[K?] E. Jenkins	Olton	20 Jly 1888	resigned
**617	W. H. Garbett	Solihull	20 Jly 1888	dismissed the Regiment
**618	S. S. Lowe	Handsworth	21 Feb 1889	resigned
**619	Jn. Cross	West Bromwich	21 Feb 1889	resigned
620	Walter Jones	Birmingham	[Feb deleted] 5 Mar 1889	resigned 13 Apr 1891
621	F. W. Hartland	West Bromwich	25 Jly 1889	
**622	E. Cockrell	Acocks Green	18 Aug 1889	resigned
**623	E. Jones	[Smethwick ?]	12 Sep 1889	resigned
**624	T. [Horner ?]	Birmingham	12 Sep 1889	resigned
625	A. S. Powell	Birmingham	14 Dec 1889	
626	M.H. Simpson Jnr	Birmingham	14 Dec 1889	resigned
627	Herbert [D ?]arners	Westbromwich	8 Jan 1891	
**628	Matthew Jones	Edgbaston, Birm	16 Jan 1891	
*629	———— Hinde	—————	5 Mar 1891	resigned
**630	Thos G. Buttery	Wolverhampton	5 Mar 1891	transferred to 6th Troop
**631	Wm T. Read	Birmingham	10 Mar 1891	
**632	Walter J. Davies	Birmingham	9 Apr 1891	

633	G[reville Duncan ?]	[B, *deleted*] West Bromwich	1 May 1891	
634	J. E. Facey	Birmingham	26 Feb 1892	
635	J. C. Phillips	Birmingham	26 Feb 1891	
636	J. Jenks	West Bromwich	10 Mar 1892	resigned
637	Fredk W. Allen	Birmingham	10 Mar 1892	
638	[?Edward] Francis	Birmingham	10 Mar 1892	
639	George Lidzey	Birmingham	21 Mar 1892	
640	Mark Moseley	Knowle	14 Mar 1892	
641	Walter W. L. Smith	Olton Mill, Solihull	29 Mar 1892	
642	Jno. H. Hartill	Green Bank, Hampton	29 Mar 1892	
643	Harry W. E. Harrison	Vicar St., Dudley	27 May 1892	
644	E. R. Chandler	Kingswood Rd., Moseley	5 Jly 1892	
*645	[?Edward] Dixon	—————	30 Jly 1892	
**646	[R. M. ?] erate	97 Hagley Rd, Edgbaston	11 Nov 1892	resigned
*647	David Jackson	—————	19 Nov 1892	
**648	H. E. Packwood	[Clarence] Rd., Kings Heath	19 Nov 1892	
**649	James G. Rogers	Birmingham	10 Dec 1892	
650	Benjamin Allen	Birmingham	10 Dec 1892	
*651	Charles Wheeler	—————	10 Dec 1892	resigned
652	J. H. Barney	Birmingham	12 Dec 1892	

Sheet 13

653	John H. Ball	Birmingham	16 Dec 1892	
**654	Henry Penn	Handsworth	16 Dec 1892	
*655	J. A. Robinson	—————	28 Dec 1892	
*656	I. Stockton	—————	10 Jan 1893	resigned
**657	Bayley Mason	Sheldon	17 Jan 1893	resigned
**658	R. H. Pearson	Handsworth	24 Jan 1893	
**659	[J. Ward ?] Hill	Acocks Green	24 Jan 1893	
**660	Geo. Sidwell	Solihull	9 Mar 1893	
**661	J. J. Baylies	55 Birmingham	24 Oct 1893	
**662	E. Woodward	Birmingham	4 Dec 1893	
**663	Ph [?] iat	Birmingham	12 Jan 1894	
*664	H. C. Chard	Birmingham	16 Jan 1894	deserted
**665	H. Griffiths	Birmingham	24 Jan 1894	
*666	H. Machin	Birmingham	7 Mar 1894	

**667	G. W. Walker	Birmingham	20 Mar 1894
668	Adamson G.P,	Birmingham	5 Apr 1894
669	A. E. Coldicott	Birmingham	7 Dec 1894
670	F. S. Arter	Birm	7 Feb 1895
671	E. Dawson	Birmingham	21 Feb 1895
672	Percy Gibbs	Birmingham	28 Feb 1895
673	Wm Henry Whitehouse	Birmingham	14 Mar 1895
674	S. C. B. Cave	Harborne	15 May 1895
675	A. C. Nicholls	Sparkbrook	5 May 1896
676	Philip Shaw	Elmdon	5 May 1896
677	Lionel E. Wood	Small Heath	5 May 1896
678	Henry Price	Birmingham	30 May 1896
679	W. A. Marrian	Yardley	10 Sep 1896
680	W. Wilkinson	Birmingham	27 Nov 1896
681	Hy. J. Howe	Birmingham	27 Nov 1896
682	W. J. Tayler	Harborne	7 Feb 1897
683	J. Alf. Appleby	Birmingham	7 Feb 1897
684	Bernard Appleby	Birmingham	7 Feb 1897
685	Charles A. Fletcher	Birmingham	26 Nov 1897
686	Oliver W. Horobin	Birmingham	26 Nov 1897
687	Edward Browne	Birmingham	29 Apr 1898
688	[Fraser ?] Andrews	Birmingham	29 Apr 1898
689	H. P. Motteram	[Birm, *deleted*] Smethwick	29 Apr 1898
690	H. Godley	Birmingham	29 Apr 1898
691	[J. J.] Wright	Knowle	29 Apr 1898
692	[Jno. Broad ?]	Birmingham	29 Apr 1898

THE ROLL OF THE SIXTH TROOP OF THE WARWICKSHIRE YEOMANRY 1852–1868

Shakespeare Birthplace Trust Records Office, Leigh Deposit
DR 18/27
Reproduced by permission of the Stoneleigh Preservation
Trust

Articles of enrollment for the proposed Sixth Troop of the Regiment of Yeomanry Cavalry for the County of Warwick commanded by Colonel the Right Honorable the Lord Brooke

The following persons have offered their services, vizt:-

The Right Honorable Lord Leigh—Captain, Leigh [signed]
[Edward Chandos Leigh, in pencil]
Lieutenant—Arth^r. E. Whieldon

Cornet—Allesley Boughton Leigh
[William J. Chamberlayne, deleted]
Hugh Somerville

We whose names are hereunto subscribed in pursuance of an Act of Parliament entituled "An Act for the Encouragement and Discipline, of such Corps or Companies of Men, as shall Voluntarily Enroll Themselves in the Defence of the Kingdom during the present War" do voluntarily enroll ourselves to form a corps of cavalry to be called the Yeomanry Cavalry of the County of Warwick for the internal defence and security of the Kingdom during the present War, on the following conditions:-

First -   To receive no pay unless when embodied, or called out, to attend mounted on a serviceable gelding or mare, to be approved by the Commanding Officer of the Troop for the purpose of exercise, at such times and places as shall be fixed by the Commanding Officer.

Second - The times and places of exercise to be fixed as may least interfere with the employment of the persons composing such Troop.

Third - The Corps to be subject to be embodied within the County of Warwick by special direction from His Majesty on appearance of invasion and on imminent danger of invasion in the military district nearest the County of Warwick, and to be removed out of the County to any part of the Kingdom of Great Britain by the like authority from His Majesty in case of actual invasion.

Fourth - To be subject to be called upon by special direction from His Majesty for the suppression of riots and tumults existing in any adjoining county, in which a corps shall have been raised for its internal defence, to assist such corps during the continuance of such riots and tumults.

Fifth - To be liable to be called upon, by order of His Majesty, or by the Lord Lieutenant, or by such Deputy Lieutenants, commissioned to act in his absence, or by the Sheriff of the County, for the suppression of riots and tumults within the county.

Sixth - In all cases when embodied and called out as above, to receive pay as Light Dragoons, and to be subject to military discipline as the rest of His Majesty's regular and militia troops.

Seventh - All persons attending on the day of exercise to wear a uniform dress according to pattern to be produced, &c.

Eighth - Arms and accoutrements to be furnished by Government.

Ninth - Such articles as are furnished by Government or from the County subscription as shall remain in the custody of each man while he belongs to the corps to be produced in good order on each day of exercise and in such good order to be delivered up when required to the Commanding Officer or such person or persons as shall under His

Majesty's authority be commissioned to received them.

Tenth -   Each troop to consist of not less than fifty-six men (officers included) to be under the particular command of the officers belonging to it; while exercised in their respective districts, but the whole corps to be under the superintendence of field officers if such should be appointed.

Eleventh -   Officers to receive commission from His Majesty, or from the Lord Lieutenant of the County, or others who may be specially authorised by His Majesty for that purpose.

Twelfth -   All persons desirous of finding a substitute to make up the compliment [sic] of any troop may do so on condition that the substitute be a man of good character having a fixed residence in the County; that he be accustomed to riding, and that he be a person not likely to enlist in the army, navy or militia, and that he be approved by a majority of those persons who compose the troop in which he is to serve.

Thirteenth -The substitutes to be equipped and mounted in the same manner as those who serve for themselves, and their clothes and horses to be provided at the expense of those persons by whom they are brought forward.

Fourteenth -Whereas several gentlemen who offer their personal services may be desirous of rending assistance towards the formation of this corps by furnishing men and horses to make up the compliment of any troop, persons so brought forward and furnished with horses may be accepted on the same conditions as the substitutes above mentioned.

Fifteenth -   All pay received from Government by any person serving under this enrollment, as well commissioned officers as others when the corps be embodied or called out on service, to be divided equally amongst the troop.

	NAME	RESIDENCE	WHEN ENROLLED
693	Thomas Drakeford Q^{r}Master	Coleshill	25 Mar 1852
694	William Campbell	Stoneleigh	25 Mar 1852
695	H. James Oldacres	Maxstoke	31 Mar 1852
696	Thos Bryan	Kenilworth	25 Mar 1852
697	Edwd B. Twycross	Stoneleigh	25 Mar 1852
698	William Lee	Stoneleigh	25 Mar 1852
699	William Adcock	Stoneleigh	25 Mar 1852
700	Thomas Campbell	Birmingham	25 Mar 1852
701	Thomas Jones	Stoneleigh	25 Mar 1852
702	Henry Judd	Stoneleigh	25 Mar 1852
703	Edward Judd	Stoneleigh	25 Mar 1852
704	James Joyce	Kenilworth	25 Mar 1852
705	Thomas Smith	Stoneleigh	25 Mar 1852
706	William Wakefield	Stoneleigh	25 Mar 1852
707	Richard Farmer	Weston	25 Mar 1852
708	Thomas Knibb	Stoneleigh	25 Mar 1852
709	William Robbins	Stoneleigh	25 Mar 1852
710	John Burbury	Leek Wootton	25 Mar 1852
711	Job Jeacock	Stoneleigh	25 Mar 1852
712	(William Harris	Fletchamsted	25 Mar 1852)
713	(Joseph Pratt	Weston	25 Mar 1852)
714	Charles Clarke	Longford, Foleshill	25 Mar 1852
715	(John Abbotts	Long Itchington	25 Mar 1852)
716	(John Townsend	Ashow	25 Mar 1852)
717	Robert Johnson	Stoneleigh	25 Mar 1852
718	Andrew Wright Halford	Exhall	25 Mar 1852
719	John Holmes	Stoneleigh	25 Mar 1852
720	(Henry Perkins	Bubbenhall	25 Mar 1852)
721	(William Flinn	Weston	25 Mar 1852)
722	(James Gilks	Stoneleigh	25 Mar 1852)
723	John Reading	Priors Hardwick	25 Mar 1852
724	(James Sparks	Fillongley	30 Mar 1852)
725	William Holland	Maxstoke	7 April 1852
726	(Thomas Daulman	Chilvers Coton	8 Apr 1852)
727	Jeremiah Reynolds	Foleshill	8 Apr 1852
728	Thomas M. Phillips	Fletchamstead	8 Apr 1852
729	John Fell	Cubbington	8 Apr 1852
730	Henry Blundell	Kenilworth	8 Apr 1852
731	Samuel Harding	Kenilworth	8 Apr 1852
732	(John Voile	Churchover	8 Apr 1852)
733	Thomas Gibbs	Kenilworth	8 Apr 1852
734	Humphrey Barker Rathbone	Newbold-on-Avon	8 Apr 1852

735	(John Morgan	Stoneleigh	8 Apr 1852)
736	John Soden	Cubington [*sic*]	8 Apr 1852
737	Richard Shepheard	Birmingham	8 Apr 1852
738	Jeremiah Mayhew	Kenilworth	8 Apr 1852
739	William Riley	Kenilworth	8 Apr 1852
740	Alfred Charles Key	Coleshill	8 Apr 1852
741	William Henry Randle	Kenilworth	14 Apr 1852
742	John Isaac Horne	Long Lawford	14 Apr 1852
743	Richd Herbert	Watergall	14 Apr 1852
744	William Bentley	Maxstoke	14 Apr 1852
745	Noah Baker	Fillongley	14 Apr 1852
746	(William Ledbrook	Watergall	14 Apr 1852)
747	(George Dawkins	Chilvers Coton	14 Apr 1852)
748	(Michael Ballard	Nuneaton	14 Apr 1852)
749	Joseph Shakespeare	[Nu]neaton	————
750	(Edward Cross	Nuneaton	5 May 1852)
751	(Henry Campbell	Harboro'	13 May 1852)
752	William Watson	Harboro' Magna	13 May 1852
753	Thomas Higginson	Berkswell	13 May 1852
754	William Reynolds	Kenilworth	13 May 1852
755	(Thomas Anstey	Kenilworth	13 May 1852)

Column 2

756	Richard Sammons	Stoneleigh	21 May 1852
757	(Thomas N[eate ?]	Nuneaton	21 May 1852)
758	William Simmons	Stoneleigh	27 Jly 1852
759	(Thomas Grant	Cubbington	27 Jly 1852)
760	(John Clarke	Kenilworth	13 Apr 1853)
761	(John Hailston	Meriden	21 Apr 1853)
762	(William Francis Farrow	Nuneaton	1 Aug 1853)
763	Thomas Grove	Leamington	1 Aug 1853
764	Joshua Short	Witton	27 Apr 1854
765	Thos Garner	Newbold	2 Jun 1854
766	(William Henry Edmunds	Rugby	15 Aug 1854)
767	(W.C. Tait	Rugby	15 Aug 1854)
768	William Lloyd	Foleshill	15 Aug 1854
769	John Mottram	Warwick	15 Aug 1854
770	William Shakespeare	Preston	15 Aug 1854
771	William Haddam	Maxstock	15 Aug 1854
772	(Joseph Rigg, jnr	Fillongley	10 Apr 1855)
773	John Lee	Stareton	29 Apr 1856
774	Joseph Merry	Kenilworth	29 Apr 1856

775	William Whitehead	Canley	29 Apr 1856
776	James Harris	Fletchamstead	29 Apr 1856
777	Robert Skelton	Binley	29 Apr 1856
778	James Betty	Kenilworth	29 Apr 1856
779	John Tait	Rugby	29 Apr 1856
780	James Richards	Kenilworth	6 May 1856
781	William Sparkes	Fillongley	19 Aug 1856
782	Richard Bartlett	Ryton	22 Apr 1857
783	Thomas Hancox	Ryton	22 Apr 1857
784	John [Hancox?]	Ryton	22 Apr 1857
785	William Malin	Bishop's Itchington	23 Apr 1857
786	William Holland	Maxstoke	22 Apr 1857
787	George Richardson	Leamington	22 Apr 1857
788	William Eales	Wolston	22 Apr 1857
789	George Sparrow	Kenilworth	9 Oct 1857
790	Arthur Coles	Stretton-on-Dunsmore	21 Apr 1858
791	Francis Spencer	Claybrooke	21 Apr 1858
792	Edward Bra[nston?]	Kenilworth	21 Apr 1858
793	William Harvey	Stretton-on-Dunsmore	21 Apr 1858
794	John Dowell	Stoneleigh	29 Apr 1858
795	William Harrold Cheadle	Baginton	22 May 1858
796	James Fessey	Watergall, nr Southam	4 Sep 1858
797	W.G.F. Bolton	Stratford-upon-Avon	27 Apr 1859
798	Thos Hancox	[*faded away*]	27 Apr 1859
799	Henry [Adcock?]	Stoneleigh	27 Apr 189
800	William Linton	Bubbenhall	30 Apr 1859
801	Samuel Oldham	Lower Parade, Leamington	10 Sep 1859
802	Thos Houghton Iliff	Spring [Lane?], Kenilworth	5 Apr 1860
803	Henry Evans	New Street	5 Apr 1860
804	William J. Reading	Honingham	5 Apr 1860
805	Abram R. Dunn	Tile Hill	17 Apr 1861
806	Thomas S. Bird	Bilton	25 Jly 1861
807	Walter Watson	Rugby	25 Jly 1861
808	William Collins	[Bul] kington	23 Sep 1861
809	Richard Stoive	Adlestrop	21 Sep 1861
810	Thomas Lewis	Calcutt	21 Sep 1861
811	William R. P. Price	Kilsby	21 Sep 1861
812	George Woodward	[Fabs?] worth	4 Feb 1862
813	Wm Martin Richardson	Rugby	10 Apr 1862
814	William Sharp	Newbold-on-Avon	10 Apr 1862
815	William Bull	Long Itchington	10 Apr 1862
816	[G. Graham?] Barron	Warwick	11 Aug 1862

Verso

817	W. H. Carr	Kenilworth	7 May 1863
818	R. Benn	Church Lawford	7 May 1863
819	J. Bird	Brownsover	7 May 1863
820	Chas Layton	Stivichall	7 May 1863
821	Alfred Flinn	Earlsdon	27 May 1863
822	Thomas Reynolds	Foleshil [*sic*]	15 Oct 1863
823	William Collins	Foleshill	15 Oct 1863
824	Thos Farndon, jnr	Foleshill	15 Oct 1863
825	Thomas Franks	Warwick	15 Oct 1863
826	William Betty	Kenilworth	15 oct 1863
827	George [Kn?] ight	Stoneleigh	14 Apr 1864
828	Samuel Bass	Cubbington	14 Apr 1864
829	Richard Reading	Honingham	14 Apr 1864
830	William Smith	Willenhall, Coventry	14 Apr 1864
831	John Cot	Ryton, Coventry	11 May 1864
832	Edward Lee Smith	Newbold, Rugby	17 Oct 1864
833	William Haggett	Stoneleigh	17 Oct 1864
834	Thomas James Insall	Cubbington	6 Apr 1865
835	Robert Burden	Hardwick	————
836	Samuel Halford	Exhall	6 Apr 1865
837	Thomas Johnson [*smudged*]	[? ?] Coventry	6 Apr 1865
838	Edward Bead	Kenilworth	19 May 1865
839	David H. Bowles	[?] t [?? ison]	16 Oct 1865
840	J. M. Neilson	Stoneleigh	19 Oct 1865
841	Daniel Strong	Foleshill	19 Oct 1865
842	George [N?] evill	Milverton	18 Oct 1866
843	Joseph Jenaway	Cryfield, Stoneleigh	19 Mar 1867
844	Walter Dan Claridge	Coventry	11 Apr 1867
845	Thomas Cryer	Coomb Fields	16 May 1867
846	Thomas [Trevor ?]	[Keresley ?]	26 Oct 1867
847	Henry Edward [*faded away*]	Brinklow	[*faded*] 1867
848	Samuel Matthew Simpson	The Grange, Stoneleigh	[*faded*] 1868
849	James Burdett	Coombe Farm	4 Apr 1868
850	William Miller	Combe Abbey	6 Apr 1868
851	Andrew Dudgen	Combe	6 Apr 1868

INDEX OF PERSONS

Name; place as written; years of service; occupation and published references if known, in ( ); entry number
res. = resigned. Other abbreviations as on page 16.

First Troop nos 1—216
Second Troop nos 217—692
Sixth Troop nos 693—851

Arblaster, Thomas, Hockley Heath 1843. (Farmer) 330

Armstrong, Charles, Birmingham 1844. (Cooper and packing case manufacturer, Livery St and Suffolk St) 318

Arnold, John, Meriden 1860. (Farming family) 157

Arter, Frederick Silverbourne, Birmingham 1895. (Sgt, won shooting cups 1901, 1902 (HAA, 232), (? Spoon and fork manufacturer, Upper Highgate St, residence: Cotton Lane, Moseley) 670

Atkins, Edward, Coventry 1853. 141

Avery, Edward, Bentley Heath 1876—res. 1878. (Farmer, Widney Manor; E.G. Handley, *Bentley Heath and Widney Manor*, 1992, p. 24.) 482

Badger, Francis, Bearley 1861. (Farmer) 426

Bailey, Henry James, Birmingham 1877—res. 1880. (Wine and spirit merchant, 20 Summer Row) 503

Baker, Noah, Fillongley 1852. (Farming family) 745

Baker, William, Attleborough 1844—res. 1846. (? Farming family) 125

Baldwin, Edward B., Birmingham 1842. 310

Baldwin, James, Lapworth 1845. (Farmer, corn and guano merchant) 323

Ball, Arthur A., Packwood 1874—res. 1879. (Farming family) 453

Ball, John, Nuthurst 1859. (Farming family) 414

Ball, John, Nuthurst 1874—res. 1880. (Farming family) 454

Ball, John H., Birmingham 1892. 653

Ball, Joseph, Hockley 1841. (Cattle dealer) 298

Ball, Joseph, Packwood Hall 1855. (Farmer) 390

Ball, Thomas, Packwood 1858. (Farmer) 413

Ball, William, Bickenhill 1854. 143, 160

Ball, William, Lapworth 1861. (Farmer) 421

Ballard, [F. ?], Sutton 1876—res. 1878 by order of the Inspector General. 490

Ballard, Michael, Nuneaton 1852. (Auctioneer and farmer) 748

Ballard, Thomas, Corley 1828. 19

Banister, David, Solihull 1855. 395

Bans, P., Birmingham 1884—res. 1885. (? Peter, of 183 Lichfield Rd) 570

Barnacle, Thomas, Leamington 1838. (Baker) 83

Barnes, Daniel, Coventry 1837, 1863. 67, 158

Barnes, Riley, Coventry 1863. 159

Barnes, Samuel Benjamin, Olton 1875. (Farming family) 466

Barney, J. H., Birmingham 1892 (? James of 23 Bradfield Rd, Birchfield) 652

Barns, Thomas Henry, Copt Heath 1873—res. 1877. (Farmer) 445

Barrett, Thomas, Coventry 1840. 111

Barron, [?G. Graham], Warwick 1862. (Brewing family) 816

Bartlett, Richard, Ryton 1857. (Farmer and cattle dealer) 782

Bartley, J. C., Birmingham 1885—res. 1888. 576

Bass, Samuel, Cubbington 1864. (Grocer) 828

Bateman, Thomas, Birmingham 1835. (Architect, surveyor, auctioneer and appraiser, 3 Duddeston St and Waterloo St; later moved to Leamington) 254

Bayles, Edward, Lapworth 1836. (Farming family; also canal carpenter in 1841 in lock house beside Boot Inn) 228

Baylies, J. J., Birmingham 1893. 661

Burt, William, Birmingham 1840. (? Merchant, 8[½] Edmund St, residence
  Hagley Rd; or junior, gilt and plated button maker, 55 Edmund St) 286
Butler, Arthur, Coventry 1814. 166
Butler, Clement, Elmdon 1874—res. 1877. 455
Buttery, Thomas Gilson, Wolverhampton 1891, transferred to 6th Troop.
  (Grocer, 75 Victoria St) 630
Campbell, Henry, Harboro' 1852. (Farmer) 751
Campbell, Thomas, Birmingham 1852. 700
Campbell, William, Stoneleigh 1852. (Farmer) 694
Canning, Thomas, Lapworth 1833. (Farmer) 255
Carr, W. H., Kenilworth 1863. 817
Cartland, John, Birmingham 1837. 239
Cattell, N. H., Birmingham 1884. (Best swordsman among recruits, 1885. HAA
  1896, xv) 575
Cave, S. C. B., Harborne 1895. (? Cave Browne Cave family, corn merchants)
  674
Chadshaw, William, Birmingham 1839. 267
Chamberlayne, William J., Stoneythorpe, Long Itchington, (Lieut 1854, HAA ix)
  Landowning family, 6th Troop Roll, [see page 46].
Chambers, Clement, Hockley Heath [1871 ?]—res. 1800. (Blacksmith) 436
Chandler, [?A.] C., Wylde Green 1881—res. 1883. 538
Chandler, E. R., Kingswood Rd, Moseley 1892. 644
Chard, H. C., Birmingham, 1894, deserted. 664
Cheadle, William Harrold, Baginton 1858. 795
Chesshire, Barnabas, Beaudesert 1838. (Farmer) 249
Chesshire, John, Lapworth 1855. (Farming family) 404
Chesshire, Thomas, Hockley 1861. (Coal dealer and keeper of Wharf Tavern,
  Hockley Heath) 418
Chetwynd, George, Grendon Hall 1838. (Lieut 1834, HAA viii; captain 1838,
  HAA 58, 66, 82, 86; captain of 1st Troop 1839–61; presented a silver trum-
  pet on retirement; succeeded as 3rd baronet in 1850; died 1869.
  Landowner) 3
Chinn, Thomas, Knowle 1852. (Farming and inn-keeping family) 369
Claridge, Walter Dan, Coventry 1867. (Troop quartermaster 1887, HAA 112;
  joint prize for best turned-out man, sergeant, 1876, HAA 1896, xv. Hotel
  keeper) 844
Clark, George, Wootton Wawen 1852. (Builder and timber merchant; for
  descendants in Ohio, see W. Cooper, *Wootton Wawen*, 1936, p. 117) 368
Clark, John, Coleshill 1832. (? Miller) 20
Clark, Joseph, Fillongley [1830], 10
Clark, Walter Goodswell, 14 Temple St Chambers, [Birmingham] 1874—res.
  1875. 463
Clarke, Charles, Longford, Foleshill 1852. (Shoemaker) 714
Clarke, John, Kenilworth 1853. (Farming family) 760
Clarke, John Tom, Warwick 1848. (Coal merchant and maltster) 353
Clarke, Thomas, Coventry 1839—res. 1840. (Auctioneer, stock and share
  broker) 101
Cleaver, Joseph, Coventry 1840—res. 1842. (Silk manufacturer) 108

Hall, Robert, Coventry 1827. 70

Hancox, Henry, Aston Row, Birmingham 1841. (Maltster) 329

[Hancox ?], John, Ryton 1857. 784

Hancox, Thomas, Ryton 1857. (Farmer and inn-keeper) 783

Hancox, Thomas, [? Ryton] 1859. 798

Handly, Thomas, Kenilworth 1815. (Farmer) 56

Hands, William Daniel, Birmingham 1846. (Shop keeper, 74 Stanforth St *or* 86
    Slaney St) 324

Harbidge, Joseph, [no place] 1831. 263

Hard, William, Chilvers Coton 1843. 117

Harding, Charles, Birmingham 1852. 367

Harding, Samuel, Kenilworth 1852. (Inn-keeper) 731

Harper, Edward, Meriden 1860. (Butcher) 171

Harper, William, Meriden 1821. (Smallholder) 16

Harper, William Humphrey, Meriden 1847. (Maltster and inn-keeper) 139

Harris, A., Birmingham 1887—res. 1889. 604

Harris, Alfred, Aston 1883. (Stamper and piercer) 556

Harris, James, Fletchamstead 1856. (Farming family) 776

Harris, William, Fletchamstead 1852. (Farmer) 712

Harrison, Harry W. E., Vicar St, Dudley, 1892. 643

Harrison, J. A., Aston House, Birmingham, 1885—res. 1887. 580

Harrison, Richard, Henley-in-Arden 1841. (Tailor) 294

Harrison, Samuel, Tanworth 1834. (Farmer) 217

Hartill, John H., Green Bank, Hampton, 1892. 642

Hartland, F. W., West Bromwich 1889. 621

H [arvey], Henry, Birmingham 1840. (Commercial traveller, Islington, *or* clerk,
    Icknield Square) 287

Harvey, John, Birmingham 1852. (Sword and matchet maker) 374

Harvey, William, Stretton-on-Dunsmore 1858. (Master of Warwick County
    Asylum for Juvenile Delinquents, Stretton-on-Dunsmore) 793

Hathaway, Alfred, Birmingham 1877—res. 1882. 505

Hawkes, Alfred, Birmingham 1877—res. 1880. (Greengrocer, 168 Wilton St)
    506

Hawkes, John, Henley-in-Arden 1848. (Butcher) 348

Hawkes, Joseph, Wootton Wawen 1846. (Farmer) 325

Hawkes, Thomas, Haselor 1854. (Farmer) 381

Haycock, E. S., Birmingham 1839. (Dog-collar maker and mathematical instru-
    ment maker, Woodcock St) 281

Haye, Edward, Birmingham 1880—res. 1883. 528

Hayes, Edward, Knowle 1839. (Butcher) 273

Healley, William, Packington 1829. 29

Heath, Henry, Knowle 1876—res. 1881. (Farmer) 476

Heath, Richard J., Balsall 1839. 277

Hemming, William, Henley-in-Arden 1844. (Grocer and tea-dealer) 316

Herbert, Richard, Watergall 1852. (Farming family) 743

Hetherington, John, Edstone [1870]—res. 1887. (Lieut 1870–1887, HAA x,
    110. Land-owning family, Edstone Hall, Wootton Wawen) 447

Hickin, George, Claverdon 1838. (Farmer, Bushwood Grange, Lapworth) 248

Izon, William, Packwood 1878—res. 1880. 510
Izon, William Henry, Birmingham 1877, deceased. (? Greengrocer, Lennox St)
    507
Jackson, Charles, Tanworth 1852. (Farmer and steward to G. F. Muntz) 365
Jackson, David, [no place] 1892. 647
Jackson, Thomas, Rowington 1855. 406
James, K., Birmingham 1886. (Shooting prize 1890, HAA 1896, 168) 592
Janett, Thomas, Attleborough 1839—res. 1844. (? misreading for 'Jarratt',
    farmer) 90
Jay, Thomas, Birmingham 1836. 233
Jeacock, Job, Stoneleigh 1852. (Butcher and parish clerk) 711
Jeffcoat, Tom, Nuthurst 1855. (Farmer, Hobb's Farm) 403
Jefferies, Charles, Berkswell 1839—res. 1840. 96
Jenaway, Joseph, Cryfield, Stoneleigh 1867. (Farmer) 843
Jenkins, F.H., Olton 1888. 613
Jenkins, [K.] E., Olton 1888. 616
Jenks, J., West Bromwich 1892. 636
Jennaway, Thomas Tibbetts, Henley-in-Arden 1845. 322
Jennings, James, Birmingham 1873—res. 1878. (Brass-caster, 52 St George's St,
    or greengrocer, 201 Stratford Rd) 458
Jennings, Walter, Moseley 1886—res. 1889. (Commercial traveller, St Paul's Rd,
    Balsall Heath, or butcher/innkeeper, Swan Inn, Coventry Rd, Yardley) 599
Jephcott, Isaac, Ansley 1868. 216
Johns, Henry, Henley-in-Arden 1861. (? Grocery family) 425
Johnson, George Henry, Birmingham 1877—res. 1881. (454 Coventry Rd) 501
Johnson, John, Bickenhill 1847. (Farmer) 129
Johnson, Joseph, Bickenhill 1864. (Farming family) 174
Johnson, Robert, Stoneleigh 1852. 717
Johnson, Thomas, Coventry 1865. (? Boot and shoemaker) 837
Johnson, Thomas, Dudley 1882—res. 1885. 551
Johnston, Thomas, Birmingham 1879. (Corporal 1883; winner of shooting
    prize 1889–1895, HAA 1896, 167–70; sergeant, best swordsman 1892, HAA
    xvi; sergeant major 1895, HAA 142. Wine merchant, 242 Bristol St) 522
Jones, Clement Selkirk, Birmingham 1879, deserted. (Fruiterer and Italian
    warehouseman, 29 Colmore Row; 26 Spring Rd) 520
Jones, E., [Smethwick ?] 1889, (? Edward, file-maker, Downing St) 623
Jones, Ernest W., Saltley, Birmingham 1885—res. 1889. 581
Jones, Felix, Birmingham 1877—res. 1880. (Tanworth Rd, Erdington) 502
Jones, John, Hampton-in-Arden 1830. 11
Jones, John, Hampton 1865, farrier. (? blacksmith, Stourbridge) 175
Jones, Matthew, Edgbaston, Birmingham 1891. (Shipping and insurance
    broker, 66 Wheeley's Rd) 628
Jones, Mostyn, Birmingham 1883—res. 1889. 555
Jones, Thomas, Stoneleigh 1852. (Farming family) 701
Jones, W.H., Birmingham 1839. 282
Jones, Walter, Birmingham 1889—res. 1891. (Builder, 34 Park St, or fruiterer,
    102 Villa Rd, Handsworth) 620
Jorden, Edward, Bearley 1846. 328

ing, aged 27, HAA 107, *Illus. London News*, lxxxv (1884), p. 373; F. Boase, *Modern English Biography*, ii, 1897, col. 375) 462

[Levy ?], Frederick J., Birmingham 1876—res. 1880, 492

Lewis, Thomas, Calcutt [Grandborough] 1861. (Farmer) 810

Lewis, William G., Birmingham 1879—res. 1892. 521

Lidzey, George, Birmingham 1892. (? Building family) 639

Linton, William, Bubbenhall 1859. (Farmer) 800

Lloyd, William, Foleshill 1854. (Baker and provision dealer) 768

Loade, William, Maxstoke 1837—res. 1841. 72

Lovett, Thomas, Coventry 1863. 180

Lowe, Edward, Hampton 1843—death 1846. (Farmer and coal merchant) 126

Lowe, Samuel Shakespeare, Handsworth 1889. (Merchant, 20 Mary Ann St, Birmingham and Hong Kong; residence 18 Holyhead Rd) 618

Lucas, Samuel, Tanworth 1842. 304

Machin, H., Birmingham 1894. (Farming family, Court Lane, Erdington) 666

McInnes, Archibald H., 42 Bath Row, Birmingham, 14 Feb 1876, res. by special permission 30 June 1876. 477

Mainstone, Charles J., Birmingham 1840. (Goldsmith and jeweller, 36 Great Charles St) 283

Malin, William, Bishop's Itchington 1857. 785

Mander, Edward, Beaudesert 1852. 372

Mander, William, Beaudesert 1841. (Churchwarden 1850; overseer of the poor 1842–50, W. Cooper, *Records of Beaudesert*, 1931, pp. 35, 126) 299

Mann, George, Stratford-upon-Avon 1850. (Auctioneer, Union St) 349

Mansell, John, Preston 1852. 362

Marks, Mathew, Berkswell 1839. (Grocer) 94

Marlow, Arthur W., Handsworth 1882—res. 1885. (198 Birchfield Rd) 553

Marrian, W. A., Yardley 1891. 679

Marshall, [? John], Birmingham 1835. 225

Martin, Philip Wykeham, Leamington 1855. (Lieut 1855, captain 1857; commanded 2nd Troop 1857—res. 1872, HAA v, ix, 83; landowner, Bentley Heath and Packwood, *V.C.H. Warwicks.*, V, 131, 171) 389

Mason, Bayley, Sheldon 1893. (The Chestnuts) 657

Matthews, J., Yardley 1881—res. 1886. (? Joseph, farmer) 540

Mayhew, Jeremiah, Kenilworth 1852. (Builder and bricklayer) 738

Mayou, C. W., Henley-in-Arden 1882—deserted 1885. (Farming family) 547

Mayou, Edward, Packington 1825. (Farmer) 42

Mayou, Edward, jnr, Great Packington 1839. (Farming family) 103

Meads, John, Eatington 1853. (Farmer) 377

[M ?] erate, [R.M.], 97 Hagley Rd, Birmingham, 1892. 646

Meredith, Henry, Henley-in-Arden 1848. (Baker and confectioner) 331

Merry, Joseph, Kenilworth 1856. 774

Mettell, Frederick, Elmdon 1874. 456

Middleton, W.T., Claverdon [1871 ?]—res. 1884. (Best swordsman prize 1874, HAA xvi; farming family) 437

Miller, James, Hockley 1836. 231

Miller, William, Combe Abbey, 1868. (Agent to the Earl of Craven) 850

Mills, J. H., Birmingham 1888—res. 1892. (80 Coventry Rd) 608

DEFECTIVE ENTRIES

INDEX OF PLACES

Modern spelling is used; places are in Warwickshire unless stated otherwise

Annual Strength of the Regiment

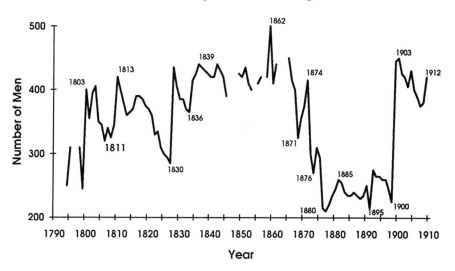

Based on H. Arden Adderley, *History of the Warwickshire Yeomanry Cavalry* (2nd edition, Warwick, 1912), Appendix C. Gaps in the graph indicate figures not available.